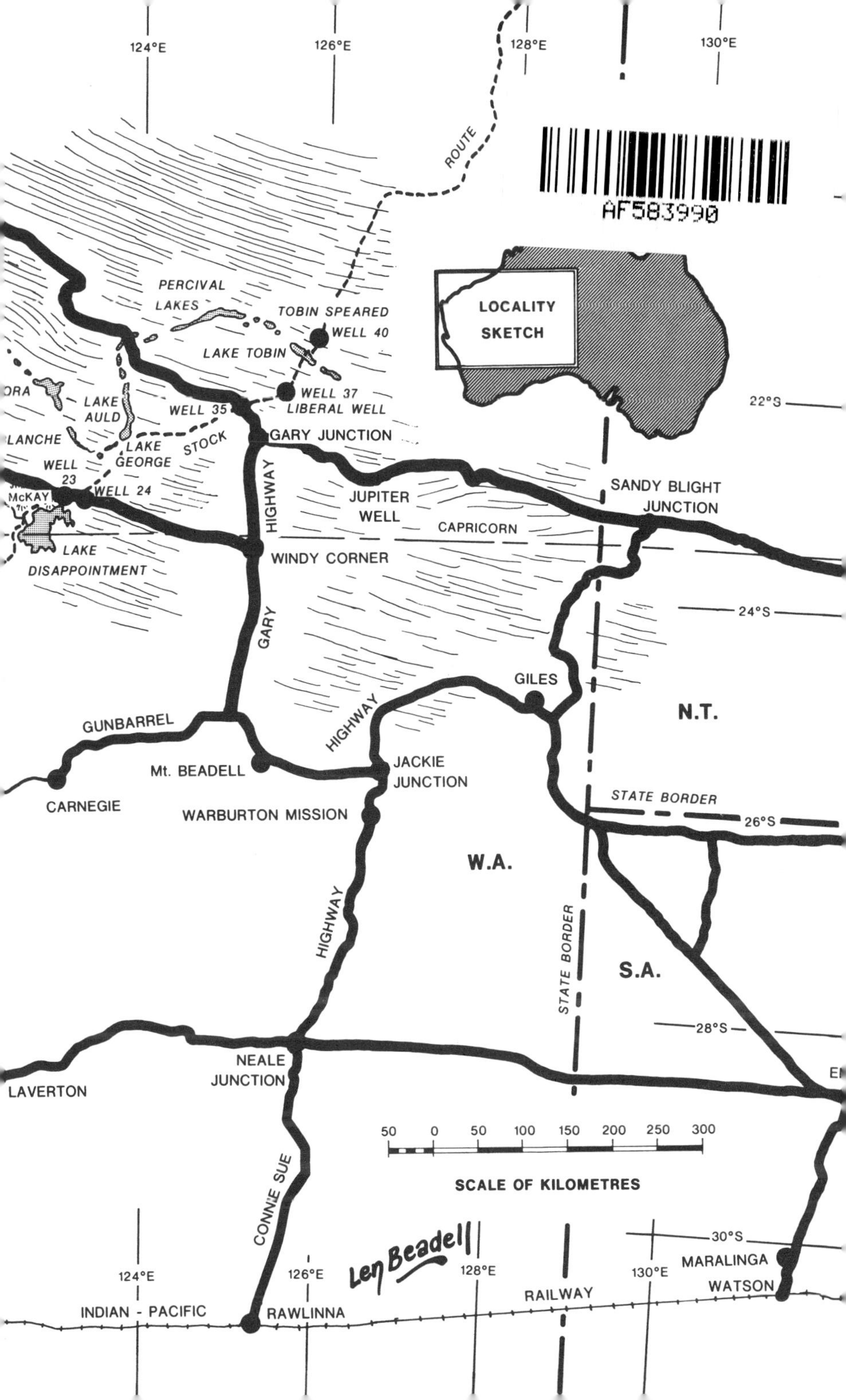
124°E
126°E
128°E
130°E
ROUTE
AF583990
LOCALITY
SKETCH
PERCIVAL
LAKES
TOBIN SPEARED
WELL 40
LAKE TOBIN
WELL 37
LIBERAL WELL
LAKE
AULD
WELL 35
GARY JUNCTION
LAKE
GEORGE
STOCK
WELL
23
WELL 24
McKAY
HIGHWAY
JUPITER
WELL
SANDY BLIGHT
JUNCTION
CAPRICORN
LAKE
DISAPPOINTMENT
WINDY CORNER
22°S
24°S
GARY
GILES
N.T.
HIGHWAY
GUNBARREL
Mt. BEADELL
JACKIE
JUNCTION
CARNEGIE
WARBURTON MISSION
STATE BORDER
26°S
W.A.
HIGHWAY
STATE BORDER
S.A.
28°S
NEALE
JUNCTION
LAVERTON
50 0 50 100 150 200 250 300
SCALE OF KILOMETRES
CONNIE SUE
Len Beadell
30°S
MARALINGA
WATSON
RAILWAY
INDIAN - PACIFIC
RAWLINNA

Len Beadell

END OF AN ERA

Books by Len Beadell:
Too Long in the Bush
Blast the Bush
Bush Bashers
Still in the Bush
Beating About the Bush
Outback Highways (a selection)
End of an Era

Published in Australia by
New Holland Publishers (Australia) Pty Ltd
London • Sydney • Auckland

131-151 Great Titchfield Street Londom WIW 5BB United Kingdom
1/66 Gibbes Street Chatswood NSW 2067 Australia
5/39 Woodside Ave Northcote Auckland 0627 New Zealand

First published in 1983
Reprinted 1985, 1989
Reprinted by Lansdowne Publishing Pty Ltd 1994, 1997, 1998
Reprinted by New Holland Publishers (Australia) Pty Ltd in 2000, 2004, 2006, 2008, 2010, 2015, 2019

National Library of Australia Cataloguing-in-Publication Data:

Beadell, Len, 1923–1995
End of an era.

ISBN 978-1-86436-733-1

1. Roads–Western Australia–Gibson Desert–Design and construciton.
2. Roads–Western Australia–Great Sandy Desert–Design and construction.
3. Gunbarrel Highway (WA). I. Title.

625.709941

Wholly designed and typeset in Australia
Printed in China by Toppan Leefung Printing Limited

10 9

Contents

Dedicated to

OUTBACK AUSTRALIA

complete with its endless horizons of desolation,
its heat, dust, and flies,
but proudly my home for half a working lifetime

Foreword

No matter how speedily you skim through this Foreword, the chances are that I'll get through it a darn sight quicker. The fact is, I can hardly wait to get down to what is nowadays called the nitty gritty, the real genuine Beadell. And I'll tell you why.

The title has me hooked. 'End of an Era', forsooth! I can no more imagine Len Beadell coming to an end of an era than I can picture him at the end of his tether. Ageless, he has always struck me. A sort of outback Peter Pan. The type of person on whom eras, whether beginning or ending, have no impact whatever.

I well recall the first time I ever clapped eyes on him. It was at a Mess Party, in the early days of Woomera's Rocket Range. To say that Beadell looked out of place at that dining-in night is to put it mildly. He wasn't in uniform, of course, and the civvies he wore—well, I don't want to be rude (he's probably still wearing them)—but there was a touch of the jumble sale about them, right down to the enormous hobnailed boots protruding from the ends of ill-fitting trousers. And as the formality of the evening gave way to an earthier and more raucous joviality, Beadell gave the impression of a choir boy who'd wandered into the parish hall to find it booked for an orgy.

So, naturally, I took him under my wing. After all, I had been there a month and knew my way around. And what did I find? Only that he'd been there before any of us. He was the original Founding Father. He was Woomera's Grand Old Man—its Oldest Inhabitant.

Only once, in fact, did I ever find the unflappable Beadell somewhat ill at ease. And that was at his wedding. He seemed utterly incapable of following the simple direction to take his bride's right hand in his. An octopus could have made a better fist of it. When he took Anne's right hand it was with his left. When he changed over to his right hand it was to take Anne's left. Then both left hands were joined. It was at this stage that I muttered to him, 'The one on the west!', and the surveyor in him came to the surface and he got it right!

The fact is, that in this often grey and drab old world Len Beadell is as he has always been, a unique individual, a character no less. End of an Era? I don't see how. I can hardly wait to turn the page to find out. So, dear reader, as they say, 'Now read on . . .'

Howell Bathurst.

The Right Reverend Howell Witt
THE BISHOP OF BATHURST, N.S.W.

Author's Note

No one can ever really lay claim to having done anything single-handedly, and an author is not an exception to the rule. I would like to sincerely thank the first person to have read this book: my typist, Mrs Glenys Szarmanski. She so willingly converted reams of my handwritten manuscript into a respectable presentation for the publisher, not only for this book but also for three of my previous books. She worked at her task in such a cheerful way that I was constantly spurred on to produce further chapters to satisfy Glenys' interest in 'What happens next?'

A great deal of expert help was also given to me by a friend of thirty years, Frank Chapman. I would like to thank him now for his ready assistance as photographic adviser and technical helper for most of the books I have written.

I would also like to record my appreciation of Norman Hetherington's forty-five years of influence on the style of my illustrations which have appeared in all my books and in many other places.

My warm appreciation is also extended to Mrs Terry Anderson, formerly of Ethel Creek Station and now of Northam, Western Australia, for supplying many details of the crashed aeroplane episode which had escaped me over the twenty years since the event. I wish to also thank George, her husband, and his brother Bert, whose meeting with me in Perth many years later revived the story just three months prior to Bert's death.

My acknowledgment is extended to West Australian

Newspapers Limited for permission to reproduce the Paul Rigby cartoon on page 65.

Finally, I would like to say how thankful and indebted I was for so long to all the sections at my H.Q. in Salisbury for their consistent help, both from countless offices and workshops, and to the members of my Gunbarrel Road Construction Party, all of whose long and cheerful association made my work feasible in the first place.

1
The Gary Highway

It was nothing short of a miracle! The seemingly impossible had happened so suddenly that not one of the grimy, sweating members of our little camp in the scrub-covered sandhills believed what we had seen, although it had just taken place in front of our very eyes. Five minutes later we were still staring at it, for no one dared move let alone say anything for fear the disturbance might cause it to vanish like a mirage. In fact that huge, punctured grader tyre, as big and heavy as any two of us put together, had parted company finally from its great steel rim in a fraction of a second . . . and all by itself.

It was midnight and we had been hammering, levering, and fighting with it since midday. The big Caterpillar machine was in the process of making the yet-to-be-named Gary Highway, currently in a patch of thick scrub near its origin at the Gunbarrel Highway, when a mulga stake as thick as a man's wrist plunged into the heavy rubber casing. A stream of water immediately spurted out into the dry desert air under pressure as the massive tyre quickly deflated under the weight, indicating this to be the first puncture that particular wheel ever had since leaving some far-off city workshop. There water had been injected into it to act as ballast, adding to the traction.

By lowering the blade with the controls, the front end of the grader raised itself clear off the ground together with its flattened tyre, and we set about the familiar job of its restoration. The big wheel nuts were hard to loosen, as this particular wheel had so far survived any trouble. The grader usually travelled on a cleared bulldozed track, but there was relatively open country ahead and we had decided to dispense with the faithful old bulldozer for this new work.

Soon the wheel was parted from the machine and rolled clear so we could operate on it. There was nothing particularly new in all this, because the routine had been a part of our lives for years but for one difference. The other rims had been of an older style which would normally let the tyre go free after some easy levering and the damaged tube would be revealed in a matter of minutes. We would then repair the tube, or if too badly staked replace it with a new one from the stock we were obliged to carry in this most remote area. Judging from the size of the miniature log protruding from the casing we thought the latter might have to be the case, so we brought over a new tube in readiness.

Then came the easy job of levering the locking ring away and the start of a minute's work, or so we thought, to free the rubber. It proved a little hard at the first try—and the second—so we endeavoured to break it loose with the grader blade. This meant chocking the front end with a log to release the blade, which was then slowly brought down on the tyre to loosen it. It was all over, we again thought, as we once more dragged the big wheel clear and continued with the simple job of revealing the tube. We would be on our way as soon as we inflated the new tube with our newly acquired compressor, and the road would progress once more.

There seemed to be some little thing preventing the beading from slipping over the edge of the steel rim, but just a little more coaxing would overcome that. An hour later it was still firmly in place and an old style 14-pound sledge hammer was brought into the act to persuade it to let go. Taking it in turns to swing this heavy new addition to the rapidly growing array of tools, we could see we still were not getting anywhere as we slumped down fighting for air after each 'shift'. Soapy water was the obvious answer. This would lubricate it and it would slip off immediately, so a basin of suds was brought over. There would be no trouble now as we bathed it all in the slippery froth and applied the normal tyre levers. After another hour we reasoned that if we had slightly longer levers we would at last win our battle, so the crowbar was brought over willingly and inserted between the tyre and the rim. This had the interesting effect of merely bending the iron rod over double as the pressure was applied but the tyre and rim were still as firmly together as they had been when we had first started the job hours before.

By now it was late afternoon so we told old Paul, the cook, that we would camp here on the spot for the night, not being able to move anyway. He cooked the tea, which came and went as darkness fell. None of us wanted to sleep with this job to wake up to, so we carried on with our hammering, levering, soaping, and straining as this task grew more impossible by the hour. We were becoming more and more resigned to the cold hard fact that to remove this tyre from this rim was a physical impossibility, and wondered how those magicians at the Caterpillar factory had ever got it on in the first place.

Paul put on a billy of tea late into the night as we worked by the light of a large fire made possible by the unlimited quantity of the same dry wood which had caused our downfall in the first place. Torches helped at times to more accurately position the levers and the 'U'-shaped crowbar as various ones in our camp came up with bright ideas, but all to no avail.

I began to wonder if we would ever be able to build a road with the solitary grader, as this was only the first patch of scrub we had encountered. Admittedly, from a careful study of air photos and previous expeditions ahead, I knew there was a most welcomed opening-up of country in front of us where the cumbersome bulldozer would only tend to slow us down. In any case we were committed to our present method of attack and if we could only negotiate this patch of mulga my original plans would be able to go ahead.

Midnight was fast approaching and Paul had long since gone to sleep in his swag alongside the ration truck; how, I couldn't imagine with the banging going on non-stop.

Then it happened! One of the exhausted members of our little group of five men let the heavy hammer slip from nerveless fingers after his bout of slogging away at the stubborn beading, and almost involuntarily dropped himself down on to the rubber tyre in among the soap suds. The immediate effect that action had was miraculous. That unyielding mass of black rubber, in the blinking of an eye, literally fell off the huge steel rim without anyone else even touching it.

The whole story was revealed after we regained our senses and with our bare hands finished off the job. These new 'improved' rims had been designed with two sets of *opposing* tapers facing each other into the ample well at the centre, as against the old-style one-taper leading to the locking ring. We had been accustomed to the latter, not realising the new style had been invented as a result of the brainwave of a mechanical engineer to help people like us. We were so grateful!

The road-making progressed like wildfire after that and the endless succession of staked tyres that assailed the grader daily no longer held any further problems for us experts, apart from plain hard work in manhandling them.

In due course the expected open country arrived as we broke out of the scrub and horizons of undulating hard ground covered with spinifex took the place of the mulga. I was able to shine a mirror from the highest point of each rise ahead in the direction I had calculated, sometimes several kilometres in front, and the grader simply had to drive towards me with its blade down. The dropping of the bulldozer from the camp had at last paid off.

Before starting this latest work we had begun another road from a point about 300 kilometres north-west of Alice Springs and trending west-north-west, reached an area just over 500 kilometres further out into the Great Sandy Desert when that previous year's work had come to an end. Nothing could be left at the head of the new road as the few remote Aborigines we had contact with in the area would, from previous experiences, have rendered any equipment useless by the time we resumed in the new year. They jammed leaves and grass into fuel tanks, and would break off anything capable of bending to make implements for digging out rabbits and goannas, as well as bash open diesel or petrol drums with rocks in their attempts to find water. The cast alloy bungs at the ends were soon found by them to be the weakest spot and these would be the first to submit to their poundings.

As it happened, bringing the equipment back to the start of the Gunbarrel Highway was the best decision for us to have made, as it governed the method of attack for the succeeding years of work. A careful astrofix for latitude and longitude at the head of that new road pinpointed its position. I could then approach it from the opposite direction with confidence of a join-up, and this would ensure a favourable position for a major junction I was planning to create 160 kilometres further on. We had decided to make a road link between Alice Springs and a point in the middle of the Eighty Mile Beach on the Indian Ocean near Marble Bar, and this route would come within 340 kilometres of the Gunbarrel Highway at its closest part in the western Gibson Desert. A north-south road connecting the two then became an obvious necessity for the follow-up surveys.

I reasoned that if this connecting road could be constructed starting at the Gunbarrel Highway end, even though there was yet nothing to connect it to, we could stop at a point in the Great Sandy Desert where the future junction *should* be. The 'T' union could be formed and we could then turn south-easterly to meet the head of the previous year's road at the point I had already fixed by the stars. 'Walking' the equipment back to the new junction, we would not only have the machinery and camp set in readiness for the next stage to the north-west, but also have the two roads across Australia already linked. After that last 650 kilometres was completed to Marble Bar, I would be situated on the Western Australian road system from where I planned to begin an expedition to discover a route for another road we would be making later in the year.

That expedition would be made possible by the fact that the north-south connecting road would be already in existence because it was to be somewhere along its length that yet another junction would come into being. As it eventuated, this junction was to become Windy Corner.

As I lay in my canvas swag roll among the sandhills at the head of the road in the spring of 1960, I knew what a massive task lay in front of us and how many thousands of kilometres of hard bush-bashing there would be to do. Countless astrofixes would be needed to guide the roads across limitless horizons to their destinations and with five years already behind us on the same gigantic project, we all knew the amount of sheer hard work waiting for us. Nevertheless not one of the party would have voluntarily changed places with anyone on earth, such was the unprecedented challenge and the abundant satisfaction derived from being able to look back on the tangible results of their efforts. Over 2 million square kilometres of virtually unknown country would be opened up for the first time since it was created, and I was sure that this goal must have been in the minds of all the members of my little Gunbarrel Road Construction Party.

As anxious as I was to continue with my plans as quickly as possible, it eventuated that two years were to elapse before being able to carry them out. Urgently needed roads were wanted further to the south, to the extent of 1500 kilometres in length, and I was forced to be patient. Not that the new roads would present any less formidable a task or be any less rewarding, but the thought of those hundreds of kilometres of new road reaching out into the desert and at present going nowhere kept repeating itself in my mind. If anything were to happen to bring our operations to a close such as accidents, or even change of government, I was quite sure that it would never be completed and remain forever as a journalist for an Alice Springs newspaper once described it as the 'Road to Nowhere'.

So as 1963 began, it was with almost feverish haste that our little party plunged out into the Gibson Desert along the Gunbarrel Highway to begin the first stage of the plan which was to construct the 'connecting' road. The point where its northern junction would come into being was about 160 kilometres north-west of the heap of sand and mulga trees which had marked the lonely head of that road for the past two years.

There had been a small range of hills which I had seen when carrying out the original survey for the Gunbarrel Highway five years before, between 30 and 40 kilometres away on the skyline to the north of our course, and this had caused me to take the road towards these hills. From each hill or high country, it was necessary to be able to have a clear line of sight to the next to make the resulting traverse possible and this range also happened to bring us that distance closer to our present goal. When dealing in hundreds or thousands of kilometres that didn't amount to much, but it was the most northern latitude that the Gunbarrel was to reach and it was from there that I planned to start.

The average country over which the 340 kilometres of this new road to the north would be passing was made up of open spinifex-covered undulations which could be handled easily by the grader alone. There were those scrubby patches on and off for the first 70 kilometres before the country opened up and as a result, the finished road took on many more bends than usual. The grader didn't have the capability of our old bulldozer in crashing down everything in front of its huge blade to make the straight lines which had become a sort of signature of our work of previous years. The benefit lay in the added speed with which we could operate as well as using less than half the diesel fuel and this meant fewer long-distance supply trips. Aerial photographs of the region ahead had given me an indication of what was to come and although these were only very seldom available, they were invaluable in this case in saving many long ground survey trips to discover for ourselves.

Apart from that bush-strewn beginning and a relatively small sandhill belt towards the end, the air mosiacs had been the deciding factor in the decision regarding what machinery to use and progress proved to be made at a brisk pace. Using astrofixes and sun observations, I found it was unnecessary to make the usual long survey trips ahead. With the sun flashing from a hand-held vehicle rear-vision mirror on a distant open undulation, the grader could make for it while at the same time leaving a road behind it. We could regrade it sometime in the future if need be but this was never to happen and our own trucks and the comings and goings of the supply waggon were enough to establish the new access for all time.

The absence of the bulldozer did result in an alarming number of flat tyres on the grader, mostly on the front wheels since the four rear tandem tyres were literally travelling on a graded road all the time. The blade was a couple of metres in front of the rear tandem tyres and cleared the way of mulga stakes in the scrubby beginning of this new Gary Highway. However the leading wheels were not so fortunate as they received the brunt of the unpaved ground ahead. This meant wrestling with the huge wheels up to four times a day and several times I lamented at this method of attack I had chosen and often mourned the absence of that great steel blade of the bull-dozer being the first thing to lock horns with the tangled mass of bush ahead, and occasionally I wished it was back with us.

As soon as the mulgas fell behind and the spinifex took over, our whole attitude towards the relatively delicate grader changed and the realisation that we had made the best choice was apparent to everyone, until one camp after the 200-kilometre mark was reached. Black clouds gathered and the temperature dropped to almost freezing with an icy wind, and during the night light rain began to fall on the canvas camp sheet over my swag. It was hardly enough to get up for and after hoping it would hold off, it actually stopped but the dreary sky remained the same. This gave us the opportunity of rolling up almost dry bed rolls and continuing on next day but then it happened. The sky seemed to open up and almost torrential rain deluged us and the whole country but not until we had a chance to gain the altitude of a high, open, wind-swept rise and in the first heavy drops put up our canvas lean-to awning from the canopy of the ration truck.

We were thankful for that much as we huddled in out of the rain which was beating down in full force by the time the shelter was in place. All that night and following day the water cascaded off the canvas into buckets which we continually emptied into the big tank mounted in old Paul's truck, knowing that at least this would save one long trip for water. The wind persisted throughout and with the total absence of wood, no fires could be built for cooking or warmth and the time was spent by everyone sealed in the cabins of their vehicles. Nothing could be seen of the distant horizons through the mist of continuous rain and although we weren't in any danger of being flooded out on this high ridge, we all knew what condition the intervening gulleys would be in after it cleared. The whole country would have surely turned into a bottomless quagmire, and any movement in any direction would have resulted in endless deep bogs, providing we could have moved at all.

We were now over half-way in the making of the Gary Highway and about 50 kilometres north of the future position of Windy Corner, although that junction and the succeeding work seemed only a dream as we waited out the storm.

Actually it only lasted two days and that much only came our way once or twice every few years. At last the stars appeared through great gaps in the clouds and it was over for the next year or so. No vehicle could be moved for days but at least we could see the skyline as the sun began its job of drying the country out. We could try for firewood and warmth, and again wished we had the bulldozer with its steel caterpillar track to run on instead of the round, easily bogged tyres of the grader. We seemed to be never satisfied.

That wish was, of course, reversed a week later when the sun had done its dehydrating task well and we were on our way with the faster grader following those rear-vision mirror flashes from rise to rise as if nothing had happened. These conditions always led to a change from the normal dry desert atmosphere to a humid moist-laden air until the last traces of surface wetness had gone and it was in these muggy days after the storm and 30 kilometres further on that we hit the expected sandhill belt.

Eric had been able to leave on a long trip for supplies, including more grader tyres, to Giles. On my usual detailed surveys in front to discover a route through the sandhills, they stopped as abruptly as they had started after only 25 kilometres.

Less than a week later and at a distance of 340 kilometres north from the Gunbarrel Highway, I topped an open spinifex-capped rise of a tableland with a conveniently placed stand of mulga trees and a supply of dry firewood just off the line of our new road. Further to the north and within 500 metres down the slope was a belt of high sandridges as far as the eye could see completely blocking my path. This was going to be it then—the position of the future junction of the Gary Highway and the road we would be making north-west across Australia. The date was 18 May 1963.

The site was ideal for a perfect camp alongside the junction, supplied with plenty of wood and a long open expanse of spinifex off to the right and left. An astrofix for latitude and longitude that night put it exactly on line between Sandy Blight Junction 500 kilometres away to the south-east and our destination near the Indian Ocean almost 700 kilometres off to the north-west.

Retracing my wheeltracks to the last camp at the present head of the road, I was at last able to jubilantly break the news that the finish of the Gary Highway was now only hours away. This of course was received by the party with downright disbelief as was normal after many other such announcements over the years. After months of dragging over endless skylines of virgin country the boys could never be convinced that the end of the road could ever possibly be near until it was actually graded and a proven fact for all to see.

The next day restored everyone's confidence in me as I guided the grader, leaving a made road behind it, up on to that last open tableland and then with the blade for once clear of the ground, over to the stand of mulga trees and our final camp. The Gary Highway was finished and I decided to name this place there and then 'Gary Junction', hoping that my little three-month-old boy would one day know also that it was by far and without doubt, the most isolated spot on the continent of Australia.

2
Two More Roads to 'Somewhere'

With the completion of the Gary Highway we were now left with two roads into the desert, both going nowhere. The one north-west of Sandy Blight Junction had been in that category for two years, the other had been just finished only minutes ago, and the new road covering the 165 kilometres separating Jupiter Well and Gary Junction was going to be made at last even if we had to do it with a shovel.

I had an astronomical latitude and longitude of both terminals and after a calculated bearing between the two, we began the job immediately for three main reasons. Firstly we had been looking forward to it for so long and the time had finally come. Next in order was the fact that we couldn't stop in the one place for long anyway because of the flies, which after the recent rains had multiplied a billion fold and the swarming black clouds kept us on the move even more so when trying to eat. Then of course we had a much better tool than a shovel with which to do the job, standing there waiting to go.

Well number 35 on the Canning Stock Route was about 50 kilometres to our north-west and as I planned to make that leg of the road right past it on the way to the coast, the direction of that section was fixed already in my mind. The location of those wells had been plotted accurately on otherwise almost blank maps as a result of astrofixes over sixty years before by surveyor Trotman, second in command of the Canning party, and a bearing between my present position and Well 35 was easily computed. So before starting our south-eastern stage of the link-up, we graded several hundred metres to the north-west in the direction we would be going later and actually formed the 'T' junction first. Curving the last few metres of the Gary Highway to the right and left, a small triangle resulted in which I planned to erect an aluminium sign plate on a drum for the benefit of anybody who might venture to this spot in the years to come. The one thing certain was that if it was ever to be read again, then the traveller would have been forced to negotiate hundreds of kilometres from whichever direction he had made the approach.

The days were still hot and muggy but being mid-May this was only to be a last burst before the cold of the winter set in, and the flies would mysteriously vanish for several months. We knew they would just as magically reappear on an odd warm day even after months had elapsed and this always amazed us, for we had read that a fly's life span was only twelve days. Their eggs laid now would have had to lay dormant for great periods among the spinifex until hatched by a burst of heat because they could never have reached our desolate camps from civilisation with its rubbish dumps in the time, let alone discover where we were.

As I had concluded from the studies of the air photo mosaics, the intervening country presented no real problems for the solitary grader until we were within a few kilometres of the head of our other road. At that point a large sandridge barred our way and after days of detailed reconnaissance I could find no way around it. The huge long dune persisted to the north and south until it became embedded in a further tangled mass at either end and this meant having to tackle it with the grader, which could not even climb it. Once again we longed for our bulldozer which only two years before had been within a kilometre or two of this very spot. If only I had known I would have pushed the road on that distance further, but at that time the decision to drop the bulldozer from the plant hadn't even been contemplated. We had had its constant use for the previous half dozen years and there was nothing to indicate that we wouldn't have it for the next.

In any case, what was one more sandhill in this country, where more often than not an unbroken horizon of them could be seen in every direction?

I had been able to cross over this sand barrier only with my Rover tyres deflated to their limits, and had set my wheel tracks ahead right to our old road terminus. Jupiter Well had been dug and named by a National Mapping survey party at the end of the road (at that date) from Sandy Blight Junction, and lay 100 or so metres to the south. It was in a low-lying potentially swampy area, if it ever rained, and the last pile of spinifex and sandy dirt dumped by the dozer was still where we had left it. We had had the foresight to bulldoze it well off the normal course of the road to one side, but not because we didn't plan to have the huge machine out here again. It might help anyone who tried driving on without the road, but as it now happened it was a blessing that the way was clear and brought home once again to us what a vast difference there was between the two machines. A road grader was more like a precision instrument in comparison.

Now we had to deal with that sandridge and the only obvious solution soon came to us. I would position just over the crest the only vehicle we had that could climb over it in its original state. My Rover would then serve as an anchor for the long winch cable from a big truck which could drag itself up and over using a combination of the cable and its four-wheel drive. Even so its tyres had to be deflated to half their pressure, but eventually two of our vehicles were on the other side. Repeating this with the other trucks, all but the grader had crossed the barrier. With these all connected by cables and tied to the great yellow machine waiting at the foot of the sandy rise, the final test was then ready to be made. Everything was put into gear after the grader tyres had also been slackened and the strain applied. Not only did the grader mount the slope to the top but it was able to grade a smooth approach on its way and once the great hummocks of spinifex had been cleared in a straight line, any further vehicle crossing could be made by sheer weight of momentum.

Once clear on the other side the grader was able to

construct the next 100 metres of road under its own power before turning and repeating the operation. It was surprising what a difference a smooth ramp made to such a crossing as the train of trucks were no longer needed for the dozens of subsequent passes made with the polished blade widening and deepening the cut with every successful attempt. We had been making such rapid progress with this road link that we could afford a whole day to work on this last ridge while the remaining 1 kilometre of the actual join-up was forced to wait for the following day.

Then on Saturday, 25 May 1963, I guided the grader driver through the mixture of spinifex, desert oaks, and low scrub nearing the swamp area for the last few hundred metres by means of the Rover driving slowly over my old wheel tracks. The day before I devoted to ironing out any bends in the survey and in no time the front wheels of the grader emerged on to the road ahead, and the follow-up blade closed the gap. For the first time since leaving the Gunbarrel Highway, 500 kilometres away via Gary Junction, those leading tyres were travelling on a made road! Also for the first time, the access was open from Alice Springs to a mid-point on the Gunbarrel via Sandy Blight Junction.

At last, suddenly, two of our accesses could never again be described as the roads to 'Nowhere'.

The next day after the join-up was Sunday and this was spent in preparing the machinery and vehicles for a maintenance trip to Giles, as well as filling teeth and cutting hair. Eric had a tooth which had been waiting for a temporary filling for weeks and as he had returned from a supply trip to Giles from the other direction of Jackie Junction we took the opportunity to attend to it. Everybody had been so constantly asking for violins to be sent up due to the abnormal length of their hair that a sizeable heap of their combined locks mounted around the oil drum barber's seat and the general atmosphere of the camp was one of pleasant relaxation. We all knew only too well that it wouldn't last with so much still to do, so we made the most of this rare occasion.

This particular place had another dire memory for us,

being the very spot where two years before that self-same grader had chosen to grind to a halt while we had been pushing the road out north-west from Sandy Blight Junction. Scotty had been grading as usual behind Doug's bulldozer when the transmission gave out and left the huge machine an immobile mound of steel in the middle of a long run on the road. Had it not been for this and the fact that we had been forced to tow it back to Giles, a distance of 800 kilometres with the bulldozer travelling at the speed of 3 kilometres per hour, we might have easily covered a further few kilometres including that last huge sandridge.

In any case it could have all been for the best because that move helped to govern the present method of attack for the remainder of the entire project. As in almost all cases, some good seemed to emerge from even the most calamitous events which periodically plagued our little party, and we always patiently waited long enough to recognise it.

The trip to Giles was made without incident apart from the occasional meeting with Aborigines who had, over the previous two years, been using our new road as an easier route in their constant wanderings in search of food. From now on they would be able to travel further afield by road but unfortunately for them the results of our efforts didn't often lead them to their best hunting grounds and were only used on relatively rare walkabouts.

In a matter of a few weeks everything was again ready for the onslaught into the north-west Great Sandy Desert from Gary Junction, and as before I was eager to make a start. Almost 700 kilometres of desolation still separated us from the Indian Ocean and this was to be a valuable link-up for the extensive geodetic survey following. Not only that, but it would provide the first road access clear across Australia from Alice Springs to the Western Australian highway near Port Hedland on the north-west coastline.

On the way back to Gary Junction we discovered that our old four-wheel freight trailer was beginning to show signs of wear as the heavy diesel drums began to break through the wooden tray. Also the small refrigerator trailer broke its towing drawbar and we knew we had the best mending material in the country for both jobs waiting for us on the way. It was in the form of our own old burnt-out ration truck from two years before which had come to its final resting place during that mammoth towing operation.

With our oxy-acetylene cutting torch, we cut the entire floor out of the heat-warped tray and installed it on the broken-up top of the freight trailer, making it better than new. Another good thing to come of our seemingly great loss from two years before.

During this operation we camped at the site for several days, and a family of five Aborigines appeared from across the spinifex plain and settled down nearby to silently study our curious movements. On interviewing them I discovered the name of the boy with them sounded very like Gary, so we changed it definitely to that of our newly made highway.

After another camp at Jupiter Well, a series of engine stoppings with dirt and water in the petrol from some old drum in my Rover, and a flat tyre on the grader, we all struggled on to reach Gary Junction once again.

As anxious to get on with the next new road as we always seemed to be at times like this, the grader and I headed off along our few hundred metres of already graded lead-off to the north-west and made a beginning while the camp was settling in. Not that it was going to stay at the Junction for more than a night or two at the most, but a measure of recovery had to be made to the vehicles and gear after such a long overland trip to our new starting point.

There were 650 kilometres of untouched Great Sandy Desert in front of us to a point where we hoped to join to a cattle station track only 50 kilometres or so from the Indian Ocean. Nothing but long spaghetti-like trails of sandridges, spinifex clad and a few hundred metres apart, was likely to be encountered over the whole distance according to the air photo coverage, apart from Well 35 on the Canning Stock Route. No topographical feature other than one narrow string of salt pans named the

Percival Lakes about 130 kilometres further on from Well 35, and no real stands of trees would be seen by our little party until we broke through to the Callawa area, which was the name given to this remote cattle station destination.

This featureless landscape didn't deter me in the least and would actually come as a relief after our previous years of solid mulga scrub-bashing, but a lot of detailed reconnaissance survey would be needed to negotiate the Percival Lakes. This string of salt and samphire flats appeared to snake in a huge 'S' shape pattern of 500 kilometres in length right across our path, and we would be attacking it almost exactly in the middle. It was to give me many sleepless nights before actually coming to grips with it, as there was positively no way around it. In fact the easternmost extremity was over 100 kilometres north-east of Gary Junction and our first 200 kilometres to the north-west substantially paralleled the top leg of the 'S'. In addition to my concern was the fact that we only had a lone grader to cope with it.

For the most, if not for the entire distance, the sandridges for once tended to help us in our overall direction by their west-north-westerly pattern with an obvious trough between them for almost the last 200 kilometres. My firm decision was to enter the 15-kilometre wide trough free from sandridges at its eastern end and to make the uttermost use of it. This would mean endeavouring to gain over 100 kilometres in latitude to the north as quickly as possible after discovering a way through the Percival Lakes.

All this was of course in the future, because at this stage there was no guarantee at all that we would be able to push out beyond the bottomless salty barrier in front. The immediate target however was Well 35, Minjoo, which was in itself of great significance being half-way along the overall length of Canning's incredible Stock Route, running from Halls Creek 500 kilometres to my north-east down to Wiluna, also a straight line distance of 700 kilometres to my south-west. What a point of importance this would be on an otherwise featureless, seemingly endless stretch of new road to a future traveller, not only of great interest in the stirring achievement of Canning but as a possible source of water. However putrid, brackish, or unsavoury water might be in this country, it is still mostly liquid and can be boiled, poured into vehicle radiators, or used to dilute the accumulation of sweat, dust, and odour all of which can and surely does encase everyone who find themselves in this the most remote part of the Australian continent.

That night back at camp in the small grove of mulgas alongside Gary Junction, the otherwise deathly quiet of the mid-winter night was spasmodically punctuated by my hammering as I fashioned yet another 23 by 46 centimetre aluminium sign plate. The well-worn set of steel alphabet punches lay face upwards protruding from the metal box as in the glow from the headlights of my Rover I selected letter after letter to headline the sign proudly with 'GARY JUNCTION'. This was followed by the distances south to the Gunbarrel Highway of 340 kilometres, and south-east to Alice Springs of over 1000 kilometres, and ending with the date the junction came into existence which was 18 May 1963. I could only hopefully indicate that the road to the north-west was to lead to Callawa, although on the night of constructing the sign only 19 kilometres had been actually made. No distance could be included for I did not know what extent the deviations from the plotted length would expand the finished figure, but taking the bull by the horns I left a significant space to include the information at a much later date. I knew if I ever was to return to this spot to add the numbers, it would be with a much more relaxed and worry free frame of mind than I had at present. Our signature phrase, across the centre of the plate as usual, informed the subsequent users of our access that the roads were made by the Gunbarrel Road Construction Party, which was in effect who they could blame for them.

On this wind-swept open-spinifex rise, no wood presented itself with which to erect a signpost apart from the small stand of mulga trees in which we were camping, so the finished plate had to be installed on an empty diesel drum. I chiseled the flap out from the top, because an explosion probably would occur if I used the oxy torch, but before levering it up to the required angle I risked shooting the bolt holes through each corner with my revolver. Standing on top of the drum I was relieved that I wasn't sent skywards at the first shot. The flap was held in place by one uncut lower edge, bent upwards at a convenient angle and welded into place by a length of broken spring brought for the purpose from the burnt-out truck. When in place, we filled the drum through the opening formed by the flap with shovelfuls of the surrounding red dirt.

The next day as Paul packed his cooking gear with the help of the rest of the party, the grader and I were away and on with the road. I had about 30 kilometres of survey ahead to plan the best route to bring us to the actual well, which proved to be located in an area made up of tea-tree flats and a prominent belt of desert oaks. It was actually a very pleasant spot and the basic reason for the well being sunk there in the first place. Such places drew early Aborigines to them in their search for water in previous generations and those Aborigines ultimately led surveyors Canning and Trotman to their known oases. Once again the accuracy of their astronomical fixations, observed so long before, made it possible to locate these wells, my own astrofixes making it easy for us to be lead to any previously known point on the surface of the earth.

Ironically, my first visit to this well had the opposite effect to my idea of travellers being able to obtain life-giving water from it. My previous petrol trouble chose to manifest again as I strived to restart my engine, and it was obvious it was not going to fire until I had worked on it. When I eventually drove away back on my wheeltracks to the waiting grader at the head of the road, I wondered how many people would be actually leaving water behind, even if it was only the contents of the bowl on the fuel pump.

It was easy to think up excuses not to leave this area shaded by desert oaks, but we merely carried on with the road beyond the well into the great unknown.

By now the supplies of fuel, water, and rations were getting lower and a trip back to Giles was needed to be made by Eric in the supply truck. A distance of 1000 kilometres each way via Sandy Blight Junction, he would be away at least a week and although we were not in dire need of supplies immediately, we would be in a week's time and as always we had to look that far ahead. Often we had to look ahead even further to allow for some unforeseen breakdown on the trip which, as on so many occasions in the past, had prolonged the 'shopping journey' by two or three times the normal length of time set aside.

During the time Eric was away nothing happened to him but our camp seemed to receive a full share of trouble. Not very far past Well 35, an enormous sandridge loomed up across our path and it was immediately obvious that the road would have to be made over it. To add to the problem, a second high ridge, parallel with the first, lay alongside with scarcely any valley separating them but there was a saddle, also through which the road must be made to pass. A gradual inclined plane was plainly needed as the only means of ascending the leading dune culminating at a point exactly in line with the second saddle. Again if only we had our bulldozer!

We camped at the foothills for three days as we actually shovelled a smooth track first to take the Rover to the top for use as an anchor, as we had done so recently.

A tedious programme followed of grading a downhill ramp to curve around on to the head of our existing road and repeating the process dozens of times, widening and levelling it into the face of the spinifex-bound sand until we could drive the rest of the vehicles up and over. The saddle had to be graded with the road, of course, before the move was attempted and eventually the entire camp was on the northern side on flat ground.

This all must have had an effect on the unfortunate grader's clutch plates because they began to slip and soon refused to move the big machine at all when engaged. Dragging it out on to the flat with the ration truck's winch, we were forced to dismantle enough parts to allow an inspection. Oil had entered the housing and we concluded a petrol wash-out would be all that was needed to make them grip once again. There was still no success after repeated cleaning, so with the absence of our usual heavy equipment fitter, we noticed some fingers which seemed to exert pressure on the plates and most of all we noticed adjusting bolts for them. There followed some real bush mechanics and after restarting the big diesel motor the crucial test began. To our delight the 6 tonnes of steel moved forward.

My Rover springs had finally given out on the dune crossing and one rear assembly was actually separated from the chassis completely at the rear shackle. Another half a day grovelling about under the vehicle in the sand unbolting everything necessary for the spring assembly removal and reinstalling a new set followed. We were almost back to normal as the supply truck lumbered up the ramp, crossed over the saddle, and descended on to our 'peaceful' little camp.

Top: The author's Land Rover at Gary Junction, the northern terminus of the Gary Highway. *Bottom:* Fourteen years after completion of the Gary Highway the author's son Gary kisses his 'own' highway

3
A Hard Country

With those two high sand-dunes behind us including that conveniently placed saddle, the aspect looked far more promising with a visible skyline made up of flat spinifex-covered country. This was in the wide valley bounded by two seemingly never-ending sandridges but aiming in the direction I wanted to go. There was still the one and apparently only barrier between our present position and ultimate destination of Callawa in the form of the Percival Lakes, now relatively close at hand, and I was anxious to come to grips with them.

The 500-kilometre long string of the Percival Lakes actually changed names throughout its length starting at Lake Dora on its western extremity to Lakes Blanche, George, Auld, Percival, and ending with Lake Tobin at the eastern end. I planned to attack it somewhere between Percival and Auld as there seemed to be some relief in the pattern at that point which might allow a possible crossing with our road.

Lake Tobin is located squarely across the Canning Stock Route between Well 39 and Well 40, four wells north of our intersection at number 35, and was so named following a great tragedy which befell the Canning reconnaissance survey expedition in 1907. In the early 1900s the cattle station owners in the East Kimberley country in the north-west of Western Australia had been long plagued with cattle tick, brought to Australia from Java in 1872 by water buffaloes.

Permission was refused them to ship their stock from

Top: National Mapping trig beacon in the Great Sandy Desert. The construction of these beacons was the initial reason for the road-making project. *Bottom:* Bill Ellery at his Billanooka homestead with its 'Iodine' salt the nearest port of Derby and around 1905 they were forced to approach the State Government to construct a stock route to Wiluna to try for a market in the booming southern goldfields there. The whole project revolved around the theory that the tick thrived in the moist humid conditions, but would perish and drop off the cattle as they were driven through the dry desert country of the proposed stock route.

Eventually a government surveyor from the Western Australian Department of Lands and Survey was asked to lead an exploration party to examine the possibilities of such a stock route. His name was Alfred Wernham Canning.

The job ahead of this party was absolutely incomparable to anything that had ever been attempted in Australia or could ever likely be in the future, and was in its way unparalleled in the world. Few could appreciate the gigantic task that lay waiting in the desert for this small party of eight men, twenty-three camels, and two ponies which left Wiluna in May 1906. The proposed route lay directly across 1500 kilometres of waterless desert made up of sandridges, spinifex, and scrub which had been reported by the only Europeans to have ever penetrated the area, only in the space of the previous thirty years. Apart from Ernest Giles, there was Colonel Warburton in 1876, who set out from Alice Springs to reach the north-west coast, travelling over 1200 kilometres through this same area. He finished his expedition tied to the back of his camel after living only on dried camel meat, and he never regained his health as a result.

Then there was Albert Calvert who, being a wealthy Englishman in conjunction with the Royal Geographical Society, sponsored an expedition lead by surveyor L. A. Wells to explore more of that general area. Two of his party perished under the severe hardships suffered in that most inhospitable country in 1896. Ernest Giles wrote long and fully about his attempts, at first unsuccessful to penetrate that same region and of his subsequent success during which trip he temporarily lost his sight, not to mention that even some of his camels died in that area.

This then was the same stretch of country which not only had to be penetrated through its centre in a north-easterly direction, almost exactly at right angles to the north-north-west lay of the mountainous sandridges, but also the party had to discover water at 24-kilometre intervals for future cattle drives.

Canning's initial reconnaissance from Wiluna took five gruelling months to cover the distance to Halls Creek, which was to become the northern terminal of the stock route where he arrived in October of the same year. This necessitated that the party rest and re-equip itself for the return trip until January 1907, clearly the hottest month of the year, when they again set off. Again five months later they reached Wiluna, having successfully traversed over 3000 kilometres of those desolate wastes. Canning had discovered that a well-watered (for that country) route could be obtained by catching Aborigines and making them show him their watering sites. Some stories had it that they would be tied up for long periods with salt pushed into their mouths until they submitted but these tales were brought about by his cook, a man named Blake who caused a good deal of trouble and annoyance on the return trip. However, upon his welcome home by the W.A. Premier, Sir John Forrest, Canning received a standing ovation when his report was tabled in Parliament and Blake's allegations on charges of ill-treating Aborigines were the subject of a Royal Commission. Alfred Canning was completely exonerated after the evidence was examined.

He had been very methodical in the way he carried out this epic trip by mapping each watering site and never moving the main party until forward water had been discovered. The country between would be traversed by a combination of compass survey and star latitude fixations and each future well site could then be accurately plotted. The wells were also named by using the Aborigines' age-old titles for them, so future drovers would have less difficulty in finding them for they could ask local Aborigines their location. The accuracy of these plots were to ultimately make it possible for me to rediscover them from my own astrofixes almost sixty years later and to construct my roads nearby as a help to future travellers.

After that first trip of exploration a start was made to actually build the stock route wells with timber, troughs, whip poles, and Jinny wheels. There were to be fifty-two watering places, half of which were Aboriginal wells, averaging 25 kilometres apart over the entire distance of about 1500 kilometres and the wells were to be dug deep enough to ensure a steady flow of water when called upon by the drovers. The ones I rediscovered were about 4 metres deep with brackish and sometimes putrid water half-way down, but others were sunk much deeper, requiring blasting through layers of rock.

On Thursday 5 March 1908 the cavalcade of two waggons drawn respectively by thirteen and eleven camels, about forty packs, twenty-eight men and an Aboriginal named Nipper, pulled out from Perth to a point two days later where they camped and full preparation was made for the long and arduous trip. Two more camels were added, obtained from the police, and a flock of goats was bought, and this preparatory work went on for the next ten days. Until well clear of the last habitation, photographers were rather a trouble as they continually wanted the camels to stop so that they might 'obtain views'.

Each well was to be 2 metres by 1·5 metres clear when timbered, with substantial windlasses erected and horse whips, except in the case of shallow wells when hand whips were put up. Also seven to eight lengths of iron troughing securely set in heavy timber with guard-rails would be positioned, radiating from each well in such a way that the water from a collapsible canvas bucket could spill into it down a chute after being raised from the hole. The weight of the 200-litre capacity of these buckets would be hoisted by the rope from the whip pole, set at an angle, with the pulley wheel at its top centrally over the well. The rope would pass over the huge 30-centimetre pulley from the bucket, down under another wheel set at ground level named the 'Jinny wheel' and on to a harness specially designed for a 'whip horse' which would plod back and forth, raising and lowering the bucket. The top circumference of the canvas container would be of thick steel fashioned into a ring with a handle which could be attached to the rope. When full and raised clear of the hole, it would be swung over to a steel chute as the whip horse backed off and the whole thing would collapse under the weight of the steel ring. The 200 litres of water would gush down into the trough where the future mobs of cattle would be waiting on either side, in controlled numbers. The whip poles would need bracing with very stout timbers to withstand the weight.

To prevent the accumulation of desert animals and birds from tumbling into the water where they would be quite unable to escape and further polluting the supply, a heavy cover would also be added. Often such water supplies are filled with dead and rotting dingoes, kangaroos, galahs, and anything else which endeavours to reach the inaccessible water in this driest country in the world.

This steel troughing, chutes, covers, whip and jinny wheels, and heavy axles to equip the wells would all be brought up by the camel waggons as the work progressed.

The party was divided into three groups, one for boring and two for well-sinking. The boring party was under the charge of a J. Tobin and the well-sinking parties were under Trotman and Corney. The fifth well was to become the deepest on the whole route, being sunk to the incredible depth of 35 metres. All the timber cut for putting into these wells was boiled for hours before it was used to get rid of the sap, after being carted from the nearest source by camel waggon.

Construction of the wells for the whole project occupied the following two years, during which time many almost impossible situations arose from extremes of heat, thirst, and hunger. Flour was exchanged with Aborigines for bandicoots at times, and dried goat, bread, and sugar were often the only food. Salt to treat the goat meat had to be procured from a supply 500 kilometres away after the party reached Well 37 and two men and four camels were sent for it. Canning himself went ahead right to Halls Creek for supplies, during which time the men stopped work altogether from lack of food to keep them in good 'fettle'. Everything was temporarily all right again after he brought back twenty-five bullocks and a mob of goats in the pink of condition.

The Aborigines gave trouble by pilfering the ironwork from the established wells which they managed to convert into spear heads and knives in a remarkable short space of time. The ropes on the buckets caused a nuisance to them, so they cut them off, letting them drop down into the wells. The heat was so intense at times that the dogs could not walk without the pads of their feet being burned off and hair singed from their backs, in which cases they were mercifully destroyed. The camels stood the heat well, chiefly owing to the men in charge: Langham, Mathieson, and Effingham.

In some instances the timber for the wells was carted 150 kilometres, in addition to which the camels traced and retraced the route with materials and only once did one knock up. Another threw his load from the string and had to be chased for 30 kilometres and even then was not recaptured. One time five more broke their hobbles and Canning followed their tracks for four days without success.

The cook went off one day to look for goats and looking up he saw two wild-looking Aborigines. He broke all records back to the camp while the Aborigines did likewise in the opposite direction. Once about twenty Aborigines were camped around the well-sinking party when a string of their camels hove into view, causing the Aborigines to crawl at an incredibly fast pace on all fours over the nearest sandhill, never to be seen again.

By 1909 the now-famous route was completed and the first drovers to attempt a cattle drive down it were attacked and killed by Aborigines at Well 37. They were Shoesmith and Thompson and their bodies were found by Tom Cole, the following drover, who buried them. Then in 1922 an oil expedition member by the name of McLennon was clubbed to death and also buried at Well 37, which then became known as the haunted well to all the drovers who used the route.

After twenty years of use, a number of the wells needed repairing and cleaning out and to indicate what sort of a man Alfred Canning was, at the age of sixty-five he again went into the desert to successfully lead a party to carry out this work. The job took a year and a half to complete.

An average time taken for a cattle drive down the stock route was about five months to cover the 1500 kilometres with mobs of around 500 head. Throughout the working life of the route, it was only used about twenty-five times and since Canning's reconstruction was finished in the early 1930s, nothing more has been done to restore the wells and they have gradually fallen into such a state as to be no longer usable for watering cattle. The troughing is now rusted beyond repair even though it had been originally heavily galvanised, and the whip poles on the ones I rediscovered would no longer be strong enough to stand the weight of the huge buckets of water. The once-strong posts either side of the Jinny wheels to take the 3-centimetre diameter steel axles have rotted and the chutes would never again channel water beyond the first of the rusted holes. Even after all this time, however, I still found the timbering in the actual holes to be almost as good as when it was first installed, proving the success of the lengthy boiling process employed nearly sixty years before.

It eventuated that the last time the Canning Stock

Route was used for the purpose it had been constructed was in 1959 when 500 head of cattle were driven down the entire distance in the record time of three months. The working life of the results of the superhuman efforts of Canning and Trotman was thus just half a century.

The big tragedy of that original party happened on the return trip in 1907 when the Canning party was retracing their tracks after that first historic reconnaissance survey trip. One of Canning's best men, Michael Tobin, was to meet his tragic end as the party reached the site of the future Well number 40 on their way back from Halls Creek. This is also named Waddawalla and of course is only three wells north of the haunted Liberal Well, Well 37. The desert had received an extraordinarily good season on this return trip with rain having fallen almost everywhere and the party had been progressing in good shape until they reached Waddawalla. In broad daylight a wild-looking Aboriginal surprised Tobin with a deadly spear and he was not quite quick enough to avoid being grazed on the forehead as the spear hurtled through the air to glance off his head. With blood streaming down his face he managed to grab his gun as the Aboriginal quickly positioned a second spear in his woomera, and he took a rough aim through the red mist over his eyes. At the exact instant he pulled the trigger, the Aboriginal unleashed his next spear just before the bullet crashed into his chest and he was dead before he hit the ground. As this happened, the spear plunged into the European's body, mortally wounding him and the story was plain to see by Canning who rushed to the scene at the sound of the shot.

A salt lake at the eastern extremity of the belt with which I was at present battling and which was only a kilometre or so from that fatal camp, was named Lake Tobin by Canning as a permanent remainder of that terrible day in the first stage of the work in pioneering that incredible stock route.

The boring party's leader in the subsequent construction party was J. Tobin, and could well have been related.

* * *

As I drove on alone ahead of our little camp at the head of the new road to discover once and for all whether this current project was feasible, the stories of these events kept repeating themselves in my mind. They had occurred less than sixty years before and nobody had been in this area since apart from the drovers, who had now ceased to use the route.

In my direction of travel the barrier of salt lay less than 100 kilometres ahead and if a way through was to be found then now was the time to discover it. I felt elated at being finally in a position to grapple with the problem and with the distance the camp was from the trouble at present we would have room to veer the road to the north or south if a break in the salt pattern did exist. Not only a crossing had to be found but one which would allow the road to continue onwards through the maze of sandridges on the other side.

After about 60 kilometres a very pleasant change began to appear in the two sandridges between which I had been channelled for the whole distance so far. Almost abruptly they came to an end, petering out down to ground level and allowing me to begin an upward trend, which I'd been needing to do ever since leaving Gary Junction and passing Well 35. The terminus of each sandridge in turn could be seen easily as was often the case near salt lakes and I drove on northerly on flat ground. Rather, it would have been flat if it were not for the huge clumps of spinifex, but as against the impossible crossings over high dunes, it only needed perseverance to continue onwards. Sandhills in the close proximity of salt lakes either pile up to mountainous proportions requiring a final slide down amid an avalanche of sand to reach their banks, or cease altogether, such is the geological nature of the sinking which formed them in the first place. I was grateful that the latter was the case with these Percival Lakes.

After 30 kilometres of a useful north direction I knew from my astrofixes that I would soon be forced to attempt a crossing even though I could not actually see the salt pans themselves. Their pattern must curve around to cut me off in their trend to the east, but it was about then that

I was gradually becoming aware that the country was changing. In place of the open spinifex-covered sand, samphire and scrub started taking over, and so often where there is samphire there is mostly the accompanying bottomless stretches of salty mud.

Travelling more carefully with a close eye on my wheel-tracks and the depth of their imprint, I slowly started on my westerly direction once more as the samphire and scrub became more intense. This was obviously going to be the deciding hour during which the fate of this whole road north-west across Australia would be settled one way or the other, and now that it had come I felt a great sense of relief. It was far better to actually do such a job than the months of dreaming about the difficulties.

I was still anticipating the white expanses of impassable salt-crusted blue mud 3 kilometres further on when the wonder of wonders loomed up ahead in the shape of the ends of a series of sandridges. I had actually crossed the barrier without being aware of it at a spot where the rift valley of salt was at its shallowest. This fact was proved by the resumption of the parallel ridges of sand from which the Great Sandy Desert derives its name. My wheeltracks had never at any time deepened to further than normal in this sort of country and I also knew at a glance that the solitary grader could handle the light scrub, unaided by our usual bulldozer.

Continuing on a kilometre between the familiar sandhills on either side to make sure that my good fortune was not a false alarm, I turned the Rover around to retrace my tracks the 100 kilometres back to my camp. The party was waiting patiently at the head of the road, servicing the machinery. There was now nothing to stop us for the entire distance, which meant there was no need to relocate my outgoing route in any way. I knew it was going to be some time before the impact of that good fortune would really hit home and the kilometres fell behind at a great rate as is always felt when following tracks. The constant searching ahead for the best course to follow had already been done, and once sealed by the passing of the grader, done for all time.

Less than a day later, without the need for any further star observations, I lumbered the faithful little vehicle over the last of the humps of spinifex and sand and was once again on a graded road. The pleasure of this feeling was extremely short lived because right at the road head was my camp, to which I drove to share my good news, feeling as if a great weight was lifted from my shouders, which in actual fact, it had.

4
One Down and One to Go

The lead out to the west of the Percival Lakes proved to be as ideal as it looked and it was no time before we had the grading up to the spot where my recent reconnaissance had taken me. Never again would those lakes cause any concern to a future traveller if he chose to merely follow the road and after a further 80 kilometres with no recurrence of any such obstruction, yet another clearing to the north presented itself.

I needed to make up only 70 kilometres in latitude to bring me level with that final long corridor of relief between the oceans of sandridges which would lead us right through to our goal.

The country ahead as far as could be seen was completely devoid of sandhills to the north and I became elated to be able to use as much of this direction as possible. Every kilometre gained reduced the distance by that same amount instead of the gradual trend to the west-north-west as allowed by the ridges, and we were to discover that this was to continue for the next 40 kilometres. It was then that the ridges once again loomed up to govern our course but they were nevertheless leading us inexorably towards that open belt of spinifex.

Further trouble was almost non-existent, coming only in the form of a broken bracket on our cooking stove which was easily welded and another filling to be put in Eric's tooth. Being mid-winter the springs on my survey Rover snapped with regular monotony and one whole assembly broke off completely at one end from its shackles.

A mallee log chopped to size raised the leaning little vehicle back to roughly level but the going from then on, being completely springless, was enough to almost loosen one's molars. All the spares had long since been used up and we determined to strive to break through to the cattle country ahead with whatever we could rather than to even contemplate sending the supply truck back along our new road for anything. We were then at a point where a forward trip entailed only 300 kilometres compared to a distance back for supplies of 1500 kilometres.

Traces of ironstone gravel began appearing between the spinifex and as always this meant some subtle geological difference in the nature of the country and one in this case which could lead to the formation of a lifesaving corridor for us. Then, at long last, the close proximity of the dunes which had dodged us for so long began to ease with open gaps between, widening to such an extent as to make us feel that we were actually in open prairies. The passageway through the endless horizons of sandridges had finally shown itself.

Even though it was mid-July and normally the coldest month in winter, the temperatures began to soar during the day and the humidity in those tropical latitudes of 20° made the work much heavier going than further south. This was to be the most northerly point in our whole Central Australian project and with nothing to stop us the kilometres passed quickly. Within 50 kilometres of the finish we camped alongside the head of the road with a sense of ultimate victory over the Great Sandy Desert.

Our sleep of contentment was to be short lived, however. During that night, when all was deathly quiet on the spinifex plains, suddenly an unearthly roaring infiltrated into our swags to waken everyone immediately. The loud but eerie, guttural bellowing continued throughout the rest of the night, long after we had decided it had originated from a lonely bull camel, which sounded so close that we were tempted to walk over and confront the wretched animal. It was a pitch dark, completely moonless night where torches would have been needed and from past experiences with the distances sound can travel in the

desert it might have been quite a way after all.

One similar occasion caused us considerable alarm previously, when one member of the camp was found to have vanished overnight. He had crawled out of his blankets to investigate the howling of a dingo apparently quite close by and had gone off with a strong torch to search for it. Without a rifle we weren't sure what he was going to do if he found it, but curiosity had got the better of him. In the morning we had found his swag to be empty and not a sign of where he might have gone. No amount of calling brought a reply and as we had been camping in quite featureless scrub country it seemed as if it was going to present a problem.

That was until one of our members remembered the howls of the wild dog and knowing the enquiring mind of the missing relative newcomer to our party, we deduced what might have happened. A rough direction from where the plantive cries had come was worked out from the camp and I drove off through the bush in my Rover on a compass bearing to search. With the crashing noises radiating out into the still morning air as the vehicle ploughed through the scrub, I stopped periodically to further add to the din with the horn. A faint call on one of these occasions made my next direction clear and breaking through into a clearing, a lone figure huddled on the ground nursing a big torch was suddenly the centre of attention. He was actually laughing, although a little sheepishly, at himself as the story was unfolded.

The dingo had aroused his interest and he had decided to take a look. The evening being quite warm was unfortunate for him in one way as we did not have our usual roaring fire with its glowing embers lasting to the early hours of the morning. Off he went into the blackness with the brilliant light until only several hundred metres away when the howling stopped, not ever to resume. Giving up the search he had turned back for camp and after stumbling through the bush for half an hour suddenly realised that he should have covered the few hundred metres long before then. Turning back on his tracks or so he thought, he plunged on for another hour without success. Making blind stabs into the darkness for the following three hours, he finally sat down in a clearing and laughed himself to sleep.

With the absence of a glow from a fire or sound of any kind from us, it had been absolutely hopeless to relocate the camp and his waiting swag of blankets, and a situation like that could, he realised, have happened to anyone.

So it was that our little camp on the plains was forced to endure the bellowing for the rest of that night but the knowledge from an astrofix that our goal was almost in sight did soften the ordeal. Even a few rifle shots failed to silence the vociferous beast.

The following day was filled with mechanical mishaps starting with two flat tyres on the grader just as we entered a short burst of scrub with 10 kilometres to go. I had already planned the course of the road right ahead to a rough track alongside a station telephone wire by pushing through this final belt of undergrowth. On that last survey the holding 'U' bolts on the back axle housing had given away as the low bushes had snapped the exposed threads and nuts, and my gallant Land Rover was forced to carry even more number 8 fencing wire twitches to hold it together.

Then finally on Sunday 21 July 1963, the road was

through. For the first time that year the grader stood on a track of someone else's making, and the point on this line where we had broken through was only 70 kilometres from the Callawa Cattle Station homestead to our south-west. It was also about the same distance north-west to the Indian Ocean and we knew that Australia now had a road access for the first time from where we were then, clear to Alice Springs over 1600 kilometres away to the east-south-east.

However, it was not the time to reflect for long on this fact and as the track alongside the line had been made with trucks alone, we decided to grade it right through to the station. Our camp that night was full of jubilation felt by us all, although no real outward signs showed. We were, together with our vehicles, about at the end of our endurance and despite the heavy humid conditions we were all asleep very quickly with no further disturbances from bull camels.

There was no further need to guide the grader which could now simply drive along the already deep wheeltracks smoothing them as it went, so I carried on ahead to warn the homesteaders of our approach. I wasn't sure what to expect but it didn't matter as even in the case of a deserted station, which had been the situation on a previous such occasion, the area had to be linked with the outside world by a road of some sort making our through access complete. Even if it wasn't acceptable, then we would make our own.

Pulling up in a cloud of dust outside their gate, a woman quickly appeared with an incredulous expression on her face and looked back in the direction from which I had come. Nobody ever approached the station from there and she asked in amazement where on earth I had come from. I told her as nonchalantly as I could that I had just driven over from Alice Springs, after wishing her a very good morning.

She was visibly relieved at the arrival of her husband from a nearby tool shed who proved a lot more practical after hearing the news by stating that after such a trip, a mug of tea wouldn't go astray. His wife suddenly recovered

Top: Old Talawana homestead—the western terminus of the road from Windy Corner. *Bottom:* The author visits his 'Lolly Water' discovery fourteen years later

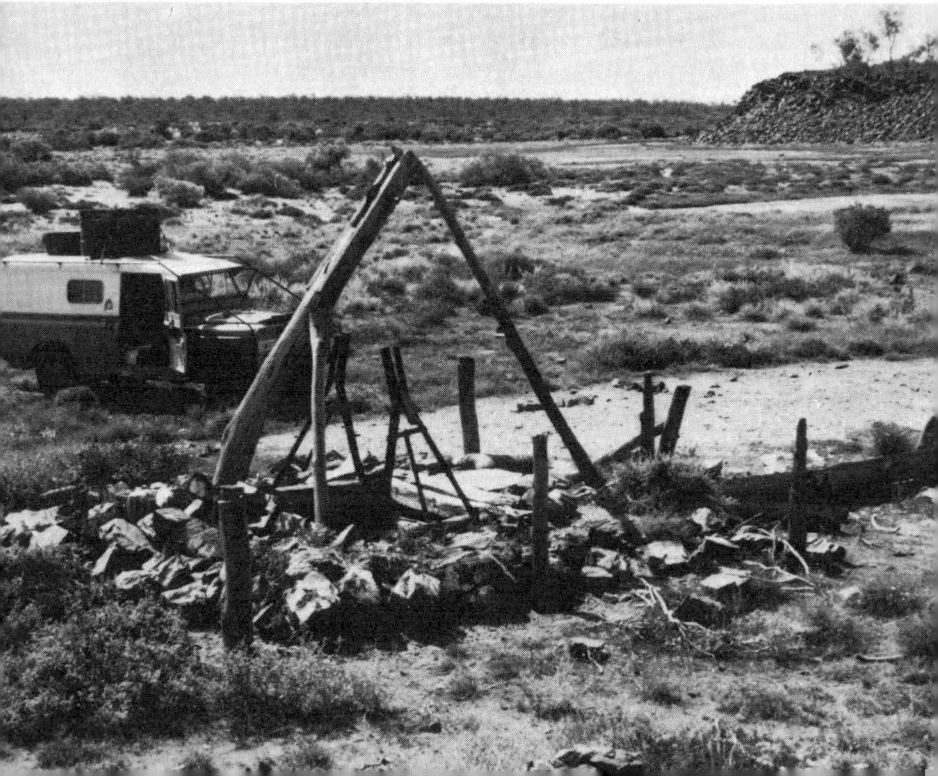

by closing her sagging jaw and headed quickly for the house while I followed with the cattleman, wearing my worn hobnailed boots, ragged shirt, and shorts. On the way I discovered this was the Young family and I introduced myself whereupon he immediately realised what was going on. Apparently news of the little Gunbarrel Road Construction Party had spread far and wide throughout the entire north-west and suddenly everything became clear.

Sitting indoors for the first time in many months and at a table, I told them that the grader was following together with two trucks, another Rover, and a half dozen men, and that a new road was now through from the centre of Australia. The usual barrage of questions occupied the time until the sound of the big diesel wafted in through the open window and we went out to see the familiar clouds of dust billowing up behind the plant across the dusty plain. The woman now fully recovered was already asking how many pieces of beef she would have to cook for everyone and I introduced the boys as they climbed from their vehicles, all looking equally as rough as I did.

The next day was completely occupied in licking the wounds on our equipment to get it up to the stage where it would be possible to drive it on to Port Hedland at the southern extremity of the Eighty Mile Beach, where some advanced help would be needed. Everything had to be restored for the 1000-kilometre trip back along our own new road to the Gary Highway, but it was at Marble Bar that I planned to separate from the party for yet another 600 kilometre reconnaissance survey back east through unbroken country for our next road.

Leaving the grader and truck which was still serviceable, the whole party drove away from Callawa heading for Port Hedland over established station roads. The first port of call as we lumbered slowly into the coastal town was of course the garage situated on the outskirts which seemed to be able to handle big jobs, and after grinding to a stop I plodded over to begin the proceedings which were to occupy us all for the next week.

The Port Hedland garage was the hub of our activities as it dismantled my Rover and sent off orders to Perth for

Top: Well 23 on the Canning Stock Route, found minutes before by the author. *Bottom:* The exciting moment of the author's discovery of Well 24

all the parts needed for its restoration. A complete set of spring assemblies, differential housing replacement for my cracked and leaking one, clutch and gearbox components, and lists of other items for the rest of our vehicles and equipment were requested by Ray, the mechanic and mainstay of the establishment. They did carry normal spares for most jobs from the cattle stations but this was something else. My only bed was in the back of the Rover and still had to be used, as were the sleeping arrangements of the party in their trucks, so the garage had to double as a sort of drive-in motel. The only difference was that we were incapable of driving out again for over a week.

Our days of waiting were occupied by restocking the ration truck, replacing broken cooking implements as requested by Paul, and even going on some fishing trips in the bay with the local Flying Doctor Tom Burcher in his outboard dinghy. Absolutely no fish resulted from those outings but we got to know more of the environs of this town on the Indian Ocean. Several meals were had at the invitation of an old army survey corps friend of mine, Colin, who happened to be living there with his wife and family, still surveying in the area and who quickly got to hear of our presence in the garage.

I spent two days blacksmithing, making a special carrier to hold 50-litre oil drums to the roof of my Rover for my long projected expedition of over 600 kilometres back east through the Gibson Desert. I needed to carry 400 litres of petrol at least to get me through and the oil drums found discarded at the back of the garage would be the ideal receptacles in which to carry it all. Being round they would have to be clamped down very rigidly to withstand the weeks of spinifex bashing I knew to be ahead of me. The frame when finished looked for all the world like a giant pair of spectacles in which the lenses were replaced by two oil drums, gripped by the vice action of large bolts which also held the hooks of turnbuckles to tighten the structure to the roof. The drums would be mounted in a vertical position in order that a syphon hose could handle refuelling and do away with the problem of manhandling the heavy drums on my own in the desert. Once these two were solidly in place, others could be clustered around them and roped into place along with extra tyres and tubes. The whole arrangement would first be padded with many old hessian wool packs to prevent it all from wearing its way through the roof of the vehicle.

The day finally arrived when my Rover was capable of being driven out of the garage where it had become almost a permanent fixture, with all its ailments cured. Paul's ration truck was as back to normal as Ray could make it, and we were able to make a move back to the desert but the first port of call would be Marble Bar where we planned to part company.

Being July we felt that Marble Bar was not likely to be living up to its name of the hottest town in Australia but even in mid-winter in those south latitudes of 21° the temperatures were still quite mild. Just north of the town was the junction on this Great Northern Highway where we had met it as we coaxed our weary, invalided vehicles bound for Port Hedland and when we reached it we all stopped for a last conference. There was no need for the others to accompany me further south having stocked up already, and for them the camp at Callawa was to be their target. Once there they would regain the machinery and begin the regrade of the road we had just finished right back to Gary Junction and carry on south along the Gary Highway to a point as yet completely unknown to them as well as to myself. After some calculations on the dusty surface of the road they would be taking, we concluded that the regrade programme would take about two or three weeks and that my expedition should occupy around the same length of time. We should theoretically meet up again in less than a month's time somewhere along the Gary Highway if our old grader made the distance without further trouble to its clutch plates. We all knew the first cut was already made through country now known to us and without unforeseen mishaps their part of the plan should go smoothly enough.

A far less certain factor lay in my part of the arrangement and again we would effect the meeting if I could negotiate the long stretch through completely unknown country in the western Gibson Desert alone. I told the party that if they reached the Gary Highway and if having driven slowly down its entire length failed to see me, then they could return and camp about half-way along it and wait for something to happen, which it certainly must eventually. A rough schedule of radio contact with their transceiver occasionally with our base at Woomera might help them to know what was going on and in turn I might be able to send a very occasional transmission as to my whereabouts. Not that anyone could do anything but we would at least not lose touch.

If I did emerge on to the Gary Highway having negotiated that western desert with the help of a long series of astrofixes, I would be able to ascertain from the fresh tracks on the road or else the lack of them, whether the party had made it. The whole thing would seem very vague to normal people planning such a huge operation, but remembering we had been working together, or at least most of the party, for the previous eight years, no more really needed to be said. As they drove away I was confident they would handle their part and cope with anything dire which might crop up, even to the point of discarding one or more of their vehicles if they refused to go further and proceeding with anything capable of moving. The subsequent salvage would be arranged if and when we saw each other again.

As I drove into Marble Bar much more sedately than I had at Port Hedland in a vehicle minus its rattles and creaking as iron ground against iron unaided by springs, I realised what topographical feature helped to make this place so notoriously hot. The mountain range with peaks of 400 metres close by curled around in a rough horseshoe shape in which nestled the settlement, cut off on all but one side from any breeze which might happen along. Summer heat bottled itself up in the basin and intensified daily while everything stewed in its midst and even at this time of the year I could easily picture what it would be like in a few months time. The poem written by my old friend Ian Mudie immediately sprang to mind which told readers that the ultimate test of a good salesman was his ability to sell an overcoat to a bloke in Marble Bar.

There was a river at the lowest part beyond the few buildings, with the range looming up further on, and it was the whitish outcrop across it which had lead to the naming of the town. The fact that it was jasper did not cause future inhabitants to rename it Jasper Bar. Even here people had already heard of my operations in the deserts and asked about the new road across Australia to 'the Alice', but it was at the post office, the best and most modern structure there, that the first inkling of another exciting drama which had taken place the previous year filtered through to me. Being a centre of communications, the building was even still alive with the news which had flooded the north-west as well as the whole of the State, about the theft of an aeroplane near Perth and which had been finally located somewhere in the desert. Nobody knew the real details of where it had been discovered, or the facts surrounding the sensational episode, all of which had happened when I had been so far removed from news sources, yet it was still very much the main topic of conversation. Flying Doctor radio network signals had flooded the air waves between remote cattle stations and sketchy newspaper articles had found their way to Marble Bar. Mystery still surrounded the whole affair and as intrigued as I was, I couldn't find anyone who knew enough to elaborate on the story so far. Little did I know that I was at present heading into the thick of it and I would very soon know almost as much about it as the chief actors in the starring roles who I would be meeting and who would become lifelong friends.

With these sensational snippets of news comprising all the versions by the locals of just what had happened somewhere in the outback still echoing through my thoughts, I regained my sizzling Rover waiting outside the air-conditioned post office, resigned to the probability that I would never know the full story as I drove slowly away to the south.

The first stop was the little settlement of Nullagine where I added a few items which I'd thought of for my expedition from the little bungalow-type store there. Little did I know then, as I scanned the cluttered shelves making my selections, that the next time I passed through here this whole store would be lying in a heap of charcoal after a fuel-fed fire completely levelled it. Later as I drove past the ashes I remembered thinking I was glad it had provided a tin dish and some extra rations just in time, for these had played a vital part in the success of the expedition.

Driving off towards Ethel Creek Cattle Station homestead which was my destination since leaving Port Hedland, I noticed a couple of cowboy-style station hands sitting by the road leaning against a shady tree and stopped to talk to them. They had been sacked that morning and told to be off the area within the hour for conduct with some Aboriginal girls entirely contrary to the rules laid down by the manager. After walking 30 kilometres in their high-heeled riding boots they had become not only almost lame but ravenous. I gave them some of my meagre supply needed for my own long trip not knowing at that time the exact reason for their dismissal and listened to their quite derogatory harangue about their former boss as they wolfed down my food.

So it was with great trepidation that I pressed on towards Ethel Creek, wondering what this ogre manager from the wild west was going to be like in the flesh.

5
There Was Movement at the Station

By the time the station buildings began to appear through the light scrub I had constructed a mind's eye picture of this ogre of Ethel Creek. At least he would be a ruthless giant of a tough cattleman with ham fists dangling from long hairy arms, tight saddle-worn trousers, high-heeled riding boots and spurs, and an open plaid shirt revealing a black hair-matted barrel chest. There would be twin chips of flint set in pools of ice fixing a steely glare from under a 'ten-gallon' hat pulled low over bushy eyebrows, and the whole structure tanned to bullock leather. He would be capable and ready in an instant to throw both me and my Rover off the station as he had done to the cowboys to the tune of an exploding stockwhip if I dared cross him, so it was with kid gloves that I determined to handle him as I pulled up between a large station store shed and the homestead.

It was a very pleasant area with shady trees and rambling house but as I climbed out on to the dust, something obviously well out of place caught my eye. It was a brightly painted, streamlined mudguard from the undercarriage of an aeroplane draped over the rough mulga gatepost and immediately the excited conversation at Marble Bar a day or so before sprang to mind. The post office staff there spoke of the stolen plane discovered in the desert and the widespread drama which had raged throughout the north-west. Could this be a piece of the crashed aircraft in question?

I was still examining it when the door on the verandah

opened and an extremely handsome woman emerged and walked over to greet this newcomer, an occurrence which wouldn't happen very often in this outback setting. She looked almost majestic in her crisp red and white dress and as she reached the gate her face lit up in a sparkling smile and a silvery voice uttered words of welcome. I didn't know what she said, surprised as I was to think I'd happened along to meet no less than a film star who must be here on a visit, but I managed to identify myself after closing my sagging jaw. My act of staring at the mudguard caused a peal of laughter from her and she began an explanation. This was certainly a part of the aeroplane the whole country had been talking about and that her husband with a party had recovered it from the spinifex plains 300 kilometres from their homestead. I was about to get the whole thrilling episode first hand I knew, but that wasn't the first thing that crowded my thoughts right then. She had spoken of *her* husband and *their* homestead and that meant that this angelic vision of the bush was in fact the wife of this brutal monster whom I had yet to meet.

I went on to explain the reason for my being here and how this visit would be short as I would be leaving there on a lone expedition of many hundreds of kilometres to the east for my survey of the next leg of our road-making programme. Immediately a look of understanding beamed on her face as she told me she had heard of our operations in the deserts already by means of the outback grapevine and their Flying Doctor radio, and invited me in to meet her husband when he returned from the cattle-branding yards.

Sitting in the huge easy chair in their tennis-court sized lounge room with my hobnailed boots as usual looking quite out of place, I told the woman who had introduced herself as Terry Anderson, about our work and my immediate plans to meet up with my camp many hundreds of kilometres east of her station. She obviously wanted to leave the story of the aeroplane to her husband, George, and asked, over welcome scones and cups of tea, all the questions which must have occurred to her over the years of hearing about us on their two-way radio sessions covering every current activity in the north-west.

I had already been asked to stay the night at the homestead and in due course we heard not the galloping hoofs of a horse but the sound of a motor coming from the yards. George had arrived at last and the clomp of boots on the verandah could be heard above everything else. Of course from the sight of my Rover outside, I knew he was already aware of a visitor and as the door opened I struggled to get up out of the depths of the chair.

As I turned to face him I couldn't believe my eyes and certainly wasn't prepared for what I saw. Where was this huge, hairy, rough gorilla? In its place stood a mild-looking medium-sized bushman with a broad smile of greeting as he extended a brown, hard-working hand. He motioned for me to sit again as he hung his broad-brimmed hat on a nail in the weatherboard wall.

It only takes a matter of seconds in the outback to size people up and even before he sat down with his mug of tea, I knew he and I would get along well. One of the original cast of stockmen who were the backbone of the cattle country, he would be hard to rouse but if the necessity arose there would be no hesitation in acting positively and with no second thoughts. I'd known too many of them not to recognise all the traits he would possess and immediately the conversation turned to my project and plans for the desert road to the east although I was anxious to hear his story of the aeroplane discovery. It looked like being a busy evening.

After a sketchy outline of my immediate project, promising to completely fill them in later with maps, I steered the talk to the aeroplane drama and their story unfolded with all the excitement of a first-hand account of the historical event. It was historical, because this was the first time in Western Australia that a man had been charged with the theft of an aircraft.

For the Andersons, the whole episode began on Sunday 1 July 1962. Terry had spent the day working on the station books, being the end of the financial year, and all the Aboriginal women and children had gone bush for the day. George had gone out to the musterers' camp on the western boundary of Mount Newman accompanied by Joe Criddle from Walgun Station, which had its homestead about 60 kilometres to the south-east. Mount Newman was at that time, before becoming a world-class mining centre, an outstation of Ethel Creek Station situated about 1300 kilometres north-east of Perth, together occupying 5000 square kilometres.

At about 6 p.m. Terry was in this same huge living room awaiting the return of George and Joe, when the Aboriginal house girls burst in from the detached kitchen yelling 'Missy, Oh! Missy,' in a great state of agitation. Terry immediately thought someone had cut off a finger or some such disaster in the preparation of dinner and impatiently stood up to meet them. All speaking at once they said 'Queer fellow out there at kitchen—proper queer one!'

She strode out to fix this queer one and send him on his way or something, and as she said she had no idea how, but standing on the raised back verandah of the kitchen she saw below a tall thin man who addressed her with a European accent. He told her he was sick and that he was hungry, which she thought an understatement by just looking at him. After being asked his name, nationality, and from where he had come he replied that his name was Miha Knaflec, originally from Yugoslavia, and that he had walked from Alice Springs in eight days and repeated that he was sick and hungry. Terry immediately had told him that of course he could not have walked from Alice Springs as it was 1600 kilometres away across unknown waterless deserts but as is the way in the outback, she invited him into the station-hands' dining room, telling the Aboriginal girls to set up a meal for him. She knew that if she left and went back to the homestead the girls would head off into the scrub, so she sat at the table with him and continued questioning him about his Alice Springs story.

Repeating his account of events which led him on foot to the remote cattle station homestead of Ethel Creek covering the previous week or so to every subsequent questioner, he stuck unwaveringly to the following story.

He had been working on a station near Alice Springs when a camel had frightened his horse which bolted and dumped him, so he had to walk and that was how he arrived at this place.

Bush people are extremely good detectives when it comes to plain logic and putting two and two together, and no amateur crook would have a hope of putting anything over them once their cold, practical thinking took over; but nobody in or out of the bush could possibly swallow this yarn. Even the most naive greenhorn might think it improbable for a person to be able to walk 200 kilometres a day for eight consecutive days across trackless deserts without food or water.

While conceding he certainly looked gaunt, Terry decided he was not that emaciated and had a few days growth of beard and was wearing a suit and an open-necked shirt.

The meal was put on the table after which time she had left as she heard the station vehicle pull up at the meat house. George and Joe had brought a side of beef in from the camp and were busily skinning a quarter each when Terry casually strolled over and mentioned they had a visitor who had just walked over from Alice Springs in eight days. I could still see the twinkle in her eye which would have been there when she told them.

George then carried on with the account of his actions from that point, as I sat in the big chair thinking that if this Slav had only waited for a year or so, I would have a bulldozed graded road across that same desert for him to use. It would not only have made it easier for him but it would have helped him find his way unerringly to the pin-point in a big country which was Ethel Creek.

George had quickly gone straight to the dining room and resumed the questioning of Mike, a name which he asked them to call him being easier than his proffered name. The same story told to Terry was repeated exactly and George asked him the name of the station near Alice Springs and the name of the boss. He replied that he could not remember. Being practical, George asked him what he had done for food on his stroll over and he said he had eaten a packet of biscuits. This was at least one correct reply, as an empty packet was later discovered in the desert but certainly not in the direction of Alice Springs. On being questioned about what sort of country he came over the Slav described the usual sandhills and told of some water he had discovered which had been full of 'mineral', with heavy accent on the 'al', in pools in a river bed. This piece of information was the first that gave him away and the lie to his whole story, as if the whole fantastic tale was not already discarded by Terry on her first encounter. The only salt water in that whole country was to be found in the Savory Creek, a normally dry, long watercourse which contained a few springs and the closest that the Savory came to Ethel Creek was 150 kilometres away to the south-east. That is therefore the direction from which this man would have come.

George and Terry, as well as every other station for thousands of kilometres, knew that an aeroplane had been stolen from the old Maylands aerodrome on the night of 23 June 1962, the previous weekend, and was still unlocated at that time. Maylands is about 10 kilometres north-east of Perth. A Flying Doctor radio report had been made of an unidentified aircraft having been seen over Granite Peak Station flying in a northerly direction on Sunday 24 July and it followed that as Granite Peak Station was south-east of Ethel Creek, George immediately surmised that there was a possibility that he could have been associated with the missing Cessna 175.

As I would be staying the night at Ethel Creek and apart from usual bush hospitality, Terry told me later that when she had first come to the aeroplane-mudguard bedecked gate she thought, 'Here is an interesting one who I will detain definitely until George gets in'. With this story unfolding, right there and then I decided that I would have stayed anyway as I thought the last deduction from George was made in a typical cautious bushman's style, not daring to make any statement which could cause ridicule.

The mysterious wanderer and visitor to Ethel Creek, Mike, was then given some blankets after dropping the vital clue about the 'minerAL' water and told that he could camp in the men's quarters until the south-bound overland mail picked him up on the following Tuesday when he could get a lift to Meekatharra. Of course George had no intention of letting him go until he got a complete clearance as to the validity of his impossible story. Already the Andersons knew positively that such a clearance would not be forthcoming. They were quite certain that Mike would prove to be the phantom pilot, but at this stage he was to be handled with extreme care.

Without causing alarm, George said he offered a light pair of slippers to his visitor, giving him a rest from his riding boots which had allegedly carried him from Alice Springs. Mike was grateful and after he was asleep, the boots were spirited away to the homestead where George carried out a minute examination of them, as he told me, looking for scruff marks which must be left by stirrup irons if in effect he ever did ride a horse. I could picture him with a Sherlock Holmes magnifying glass and torch studying the boots and thus adding more ammunition to his suspicions, which was really the main reason for his thinking of the slippers in the first place. This went on well after all the rotor arms and firearms had been removed from all the station vehicles, so no 'midnight flit' could take place. Efforts were then made to contact Constable Ward at Nullagine but he could not be contacted until the following morning and after this was done the police officer arrived at Ethel Creek just before noon on Monday 2 July.

In order that a close watch could be kept on him, Mike had been casually asked on that morning if he would like to help transplant onions in the station vegetable garden. Here Constable Ward was led on arrival and conducted the first official interview. The Yugoslav only repeated the same old story as he had told twice the previous evening. Norman Ward then telephoned to Meekatharra and contacted Inspector Sunter who was there investigating the missing aircraft and he in turn rang Perth. Things then began to happen in quick succession and the next morning two detectives arrived at the station by air closely followed by a Press plane. The detectives, Detective Sergeant L. Spargo and Detective Max Baker, agreed to have the Press photograph Mike. An apparatus to transmit photographs had been set up at a place called Mundiwindi, 130 kilometres south of Ethel Creek, and the picture was flashed to Perth where it appeared that same afternoon in the *Daily News*. The heading for the item was 'The Man from Nowhere'.

The manager of the Rex Aviation Company who owned the stolen Cessna, John Benson, was the pilot who volunteered to fly the detectives up to Ethel Creek but he had to stop overnight at Meekatharra on the long flight north. On release of the Perth *Daily News*, several people immediately identified the photograph as being that of a Milan Iskra who had been working at a foundry near Perth. That had been enough for the detectives who together with the so-called 'Mike' took off in the Rex Aviation plane for Perth, followed by the chartered Press aircraft, stopping again overnight in Meekatharra. Mike spent the evening in the local jail there, because by then it was obvious he had a lot to hide, beginning with using a false name. Of course everyone at this stage was sure that at least the pilot of the stolen plane had been found, and Terry and George could at last voice what they had known since first seeing him, without fear of ridicule from fellow bushman. Once anybody in the Australian outback says or does anything at all out of place like that, the entire country knows about it immediately and he virtually never hears the end of it. All in good but 'serious' fun of course.

Little did Mike, or as we now had to refer to him as Milan Iskra, know how unlucky he was to happen into Ethel Creek, not knowing that George Anderson's brother was actually Inspector A. F. (Bert) Anderson. Stationed at Broome, Bert was in charge of the whole of the Roebourne–Kimberley police district, and it wasn't long before he was in the thick of it at Ethel Creek. Bert was a very experienced bushman and came down to the scene with Constable Graysmark from Broome, and with his brother George and two Aborigines 'Shovel Shovel' and 'Left Hand Jumbo' as trackers, left Ethel Creek for the desert after a portable radio report from a previous search party. Already Constable Ward and Joe Criddle, the owner of the adjoining Walgun Station to the south-east, had headed off with several trackers to back track the mystery man's footprints, but their vehicle was totally unsuitable to negotiate the sandhills in the desert and they had reported this to Ethel Creek over their transceiver.

At a small well, named Cockatina, Bert and his party camped with Joe's original group. The plan was then decided upon for the Inspector with one Aboriginal to track on foot and the other tracker would carry on with Constable Graysmark, while George drove the vehicle, a 1-tonne jeep. This was forced to travel long distances to find crossings on the high sandhills and then describe

Inspector Bert Anderson

huge half circles to pick up the tracking pair and the fresh pair would then take over. The vehicle would be off again finding crossings and so the pattern of the search continued on and on into the remote desert south-east of Ethel Creek towards the Savory Creek and the 'minerAL' water.

The Aborigines had of course first been shown the shoes belonging to the mystery man and they noted the heel of one had a metal plate and the other had not. This made the tracks quite distinctive and what was a normally easy job for the well-known skills of Aboriginal trackers was made even easier, but nevertheless the search had to proceed at the earliest possible time while the tracks were at their freshest and not obliterated by wind over the sand.

Bert's party travelled using this same procedure for eight days at the speed of a few kilometres per hour, and never once lost the fading tracks. The trackers read into the tracks that their man had staggered up the 40-metre high sandridges and had slid down again, had drunk brackish water, and had eaten frugally from his packet of biscuits. Iskra had been able to keep to a good north-westerly line during the day by use of a wrist-compass but the Aborigines saw where he had attempted to carry on at night and had wandered about, falling over spiky clumps of spinifex and blundering into small shrubs. This proved the wisdom of their method of tracking on foot as being the only way possible to conduct such a search.

For once I was sorry to hear that the evening meal was ready, as I was by now sitting on the edge of the big chair, hobnailed boots tucked under instead of their usual position outstretched with their steel heels damaging the floor. George had, after all, been out all day and was hungry, not to mention the fact that I hadn't eaten properly since leaving Marble Bar, so the really welcomed food arrived from the same separate kitchen in which all this tableau had begun. I considered myself lucky that the same Aboriginal girls hadn't been the first to see me when I dragged myself in earlier that day, instead of Terry. They would probably have 'gone bush properly' this time!

At last we were able to resume our places in the living

room, a feature of which was an enormous felt-backed wall-panel displaying thousands of silver souvenir spoons from almost everywhere on earth. This was partly explained by the fact that Terry originally came from Ireland, where she would have undoubtedly been one of the legendary 'Wild Irish Roses'. It was a wonder how she escaped the shamrock country in the first place and found her way to Ethel Creek and George. Eventually the fantastic story proceeded.

Towards the end of the eighth day Bert Anderson's party was getting to the point of no return, owing to the shortage of petrol, for the vehicle had frequently become bogged and had been dug out at the expense of the limited fuel carried. These men would carry on despite diminishing food and extreme conditions but whatever they were personally prepared to do, the petrol ultimately governed their range from the homestead.

Then on the afternoon of Friday 13 July just as they were deciding on a turn around, the tracks led over a high sandridge and from the top, the tired but elated trackers

"Scuse me boss, what SORT of aircraft was it again?"

saw an aeroplane standing on its nose in the intervening spinifex flat. On reaching it as fast as their heavy boots could carry them, they saw that the wings and fuselage were crumpled and the front wheel on the tricycle undercarriage had been ripped off. The ground marks indicated that the aircraft had come in from the east and skimmed down between the parallel sandridges, slamming into the ground heavily and wrenching off the wheel which was buried in the sand.

Although the search party had enough water, they had lived on salt beef and damper, camping at night in the freezing temperatures of mid-winter, but they all conceded that theirs was nothing compared with the incredible feat enacted only a fortnight before by Milan Iskra. He had actually walked (if not from Alice Springs), an astounding distance of over 300 kilometres in just over a week. As well as the wrist-compass he had a small torch, the batteries of which gave out, explaining the reason for his wandering off course during the cold black nights. A box of matches were found near the plane, so he was not even able to light a fire for warmth. And all this after surviving a plane crash!

6
Back to the Bush

Only about thirty years of age, Milan Iskra had one burning ambition and that was to get back to Yugoslavia as soon as he could using any means available to him, legal or illegal. Known already to a Perth psychiatrist who later described him as being a schizophrenic who although often pretending to lose his memory, still recognised acts of right and wrong.

He first arrived in Australia in 1956 when, living in Melbourne, he received a flying lesson for which he paid an amount equivalent to about a dollar. This was discovered after an inspection of two diaries found on him by George Anderson, one of which was sewn into the lining of his jacket. Some of the writing was in his own language but another item in English disclosed he once worked only 200 kilometres north-west of Ethel Creek at the Australian Blue Asbestos Mine at Wittenoom Gorge, before moving to Perth to work in a foundry. He remembered nothing of the people mentioned in the diary with whom he came in contact before embarking on this latest spectacular adventure from his last known address of Hay Street in Perth.

So it was that on the night of 23 June 1962, Iskra made his way to Maylands where he broke into the warehouse of Rex Aviation Ltd and stole a Cessna 175 aircraft valued then at about $16 000. Systematically syphoning 110 litres of petrol from other planes he prepared for his attempted flight half-way across the world to Yugoslavia—all with the one-dollar flying lesson six years before to help him.

According to Terry he later revealed he had no idea of just how 'thick' Australia was, but he knew how 'fat' it was coming from Melbourne, and on this evening he thought that he would be clear over the northern coastline in an hour or so and well on his way overseas.

The dozens of impossible hurdles including radar trackers, the gigantic search which would certainly follow the discovery of the theft, and the hoped for unannounced landings in foreign countries didn't seem to have entered his mind. Nobody in his right mind could ever hope to accomplish such an impossible feat with the little money found on him, but that must have been the point. Only a person not in possession of all his faculties, however

Milan Iskra

obsessed with reaching a goal, would think twice about such a course of action doomed to certain failure from the start.

He reasoned he'd need water for his journey, so he also stole two plastic water bottles and as an aid to navigation added two aircraft maps to help him. His wrist-compass was a brilliant thought which undoubtedly saved his life as events were to prove, although at that time he probably brought it along to find his house in Europe on arrival.

After collecting the articles considered necessary for the planned trip, Iskra somehow started the single engine on the plane and taxied out on to the unlit runway. As he was taught by the instructor during his lesson, he revved up and actually became airborne without hitting some obstacle in the darkness. It was in reality a very skilful accomplishment and not one to be recommended by the Department of Civil Aviation to even an accomplished pilot, but here was this diminutive 171-centimetre New Australian merrily on the way to his homeland flying north.

Daylight came very soon after take-off and the world must have looked very good to Iskra as he flew over the spinifex, made silver by the low angle of the early morning sun. In due course he passed over the Wiluna area where the Canning Stock Route starts its long snake-like path to Halls Creek and this should have alarmed him to see from his maps he was only one-third of the way to Australia's northern coastline. In his mind at the outset he reckoned on being already clear of the mainland by then.

On and on he flew, crossing over the stock route probably without even seeing it, after passing within earshot of the Granite Peak Station homestead who reported the fact on their next Flying Doctor radio sked.

From then on he was in real outback no-man's land flying over almost 1000 kilometres of red sandridge and spinifex country as stark and featureless as any to be seen in outback Australia. He had come to the western fringe of the Gibson Desert, but then only 150 kilometres into this area as it so happened.

Although gallant in its attempt, the solitary little engine

still needed fuel to keep it going and as the tanks in the wings drained, it began to splutter and miss-fire until no drops were left to splash into the petrol lines and it finally gave up. No one could know the thoughts going through Iskra's head at that instant, but it wouldn't be very hard to guess. All his dreams of landing safely in Yugoslavia crumbled in an instant, leaving him with one main substitute objective and that was to get out of this situation alive.

Owing to the direction of the parallel sandridges which he was crossing at right angles, he circled to the left and glided down into the nearest intervening valley strewn with metre-high hummocks of spinifex. As the tell-tale markings on the ground revealed the rest of the story to Bert and his party, the plane ricochetted from one to the other in what must have taken the prize for the roughest landing, until the nose wheel tore off and the plane came to a most ungainly stop on its nose.

Ever practical to the last, Iskra must have concluded that this was something to break the monotony if nothing else, as it had at least not broken every bone in his body. Climbing out of the cockpit must have been quite an interesting manoeuvre to say the least and after slithering down into the spikey foliage, undoubtedly hoping the whole thing wasn't about to explode, the unfortunate would-be international air traveller was faced with taking stock of his situation. From his maps and rough dead reckoning from the Wiluna area as to his location, he realised he had a huge job on his hands and immediately started his trek in the only sensible direction to the nearest help. The wrist-compass was a real brainwave, keeping him to his north-west plotted direction towards Ethel Creek Station, clutching a water bottle and his packet of biscuits.

In less than 100 kilometres he came to the Savory Creek with its give-away 'minerAL' water springs and the first European he saw since leaving Perth was Terry Anderson, 150 kilometres in a straight line further on. His nightly wanderings and deviations added many kilometres to that figure and there must have been many times during the week following the crash that he might have been ready to accept defeat and death in the desert from sheer hunger and thirst. If this whole episode had been enacted during the summer months, he quite surely would have dropped in his tracks within a couple of days, a victim of the savage heat in a waterless desert. As it was he was resourceful enough to attempt extracting sap from herbage but the bush he tried was a tree balsam, the milky fluid from which made him very sick and almost poisoned him on the spot.

After I pieced this incredible story together at Ethel Creek, I couldn't help feeling an immense admiration for Milan Iskra in spite of the fact that he had been guilty of a major crime, causing the police and everyone concerned weeks of expensive and time-consuming work. If a similar achievement had been perpetrated behind enemy lines in a war, the soldier would have been highly decorated and acclaimed as a hero. As it was, not too many people—bushmen or trained soldiers—could have been capable of succeeding in such an exploit unless they were, for a start, 100 per cent physically fit.

During the subsequent and inevitable trial in Perth, George flatly refused to attend the court until his brother Inspector Bert Anderson threatened to subpoena him. He finally and begrudgingly came down from Ethel Creek and was forced to substitute his riding trousers and spurs for a suit and tie.

The whole unbelievable explanation of an aircraft's mudguard perched innocently on the homestead gatepost had at last come to an end. I hadn't seen my Rover outside since climbing out of it that same afternoon, but it was time to call a halt to this eventful day as bush people generally start nodding much earlier in the evening than their city cousins. I didn't have to go out for my swag as Terry had already made a bed up on the verandah to which I gratefully wended my way at this late hour, my mind still reeling with the happenings of the day. The last thing I reflected upon before falling into oblivion was that this was the first real bed I'd slept in for many months.

First light next morning seemed to be upon us in an

instant and regardless of the lateness of the evening we were all up well before the sun and ready for the new day in the bush. I had to be on my way out into the unknown western Gibson Desert as I knew there was 600 kilometres of desolate country waiting for me to traverse and reach our Gary Highway in time to meet the rest of my party returning on the road we had just made to Callawa.

The subject of the sacked station hands cropped up over breakfast and it seems they had been making a nuisance of themselves to the Aboriginal girls in the kitchen, even after repeated warnings from George, who was quite justified in sending them packing. As it happened, I could have done with the food I had given to them in the weeks to come in the desert but I didn't mention my feeding them after hearing the reason for their eviction.

The Andersons had become quite concerned about my projected expedition especially as I was to attempt it on my own. I assured them I'd been doing nothing else for the last decade in that country and it was just another routine operation using astrofixes for navigation, a feature which didn't impress George at all. Before finally preparing the Rover with extra fuel and water, George took me on an inspection of the station environs and the wheeltracks which would lead me to Walgun Station where Joe Criddle lived, on the way to my plotted starting point past yet another homestead called Billanooka owned by Bill Ellery. I had yet to see these but I knew Billanooka to be the most remote and easterly station in those latitudes, trailing off vaguely into the Gibson Desert.

Back at Ethel Creek we hoisted up on to the Rover's reinforced roof two more old oil drums of petrol, binding it to the others already there with two stirrup iron straps which I bought from the large store shed I'd seen on first pulling into the station. There was no room for anything else weight-wise to the already grossly overloaded vehicle but we all knew the fuel would be going down at a great rate with every kilometre travelled.

To show the personal concern George felt and just as I was in the Rover about to drive off, he stopped me to say he'd like to see another 18-litre tin of petrol tied on to the bonnet to 'use up first'. There was a space unused in front of the windscreen so with another stirrup strap, the tin was duly lashed to my scrub-bashing rods and after a last farewell, both of us knowing that I'd be back when we'd finished the road, I slowly lumbered away towards Joe's homestead to the south-east. Although I did not know it at that moment, 18 litres of fuel was all I finished up with when I eventually broke through to the Gary Highway and without it I would definitely have been lucky to make it. At the very least I would have been thinking hard about how far I'd have to walk as the other 400 litres of petrol came to its end.

Joe Criddle already knew of my coming from his transceiver and the Aborigines around Walgun already had the homestead gate open as I drove the burdened vehicle slowly through. I was surprised at the neatness of his house both inside and out after having the midday meal with him. Glass-fronted cupboards and ornaments seemed out of place in this wild country and delicately carved emu eggs hung from the walls, done by one of his Aboriginal artists with a horseshoe nail. Buckjumping horses and animals were depicted among the intricate patterns and I knew that few people could have done them so perfectly. One even showed a Flying Doctor aeroplane in flight over the spinifex, the shape of which came from a *Stock and Station* magazine.

We talked briefly about Joe's part in the tracking of Iskra until it was time to be on the move again and we also knew we'd see each other when and if I got through and made the road link.

Another 50 kilometres saw my little Land Rover approaching the last habitation I'd be seeing for a long time in the shape of Billanooka. In contrast, Bill Ellery's 'homestead' was something to be seen to be believed.

At first glance as I drove slowly across the dusty flat towards the semi-circular tin shed, the whole place appeared to be deserted but an old man emerged from behind a screened section of a windmill tower on hearing the approaching motor. He was tall and very thin and wore the usual outback uniform of riding trousers and boots, checkered shirt, and wide-brimmed hat. A shock of white beard hid most of his face and I thought I was about to finally meet up with Bill Ellery. Not so, as I discovered after climbing out of the Rover to learn this was only a visitor. He must have been over eighty and told me that Bill would be along soon, after putting on a billy for a drink of tea. To do this we had to bend double under an array of hanging saddles with dangling stirrups, hurricane lamp, hobble chains, water bags, and edge past iron waggon tyres, all of which were on the verandah.

The 'verandah' was of Bill's special design, being an extension of the hut by merely stringing wire netting over bush post uprights and covering it with spinifex. Any few drops of rain which might fall every year or so in this most desolate area would come straight through to the dirt floor which carried on into the building. This was the hut whose doorway would easily admit a small boy but anyone else was forced to remain in the same doubled-over position to clear the log at the top. It was explained away by Bill later that in the beginning the door was of normal height but this gradually reduced as the white ants ate the bottoms off the posts.

It was impossible to see anything inside coming from the glare of the desert but after a spell of groping about in the darkness, my eyes slowly made out an old bed and a wood stove on which was a billy of bore water. The fire helped to see the surrounding eating place as it came to life and the rough bush wood table, tin of treacle, bottle of tomato sauce, and a new green cardboard box of salt. Before the water boiled we heard the rattle of a truck coming from a nearby dam and I knew that this would have to be Bill.

Going out again to meet him I almost broke my face on the low door frame in the semi-darkness and again ran the gauntlet of the verandah obstacles to the wire fence. Old Bill forced himself out from behind the steering wheel, being the exact opposite build of the 'visitor', and teetered over to me on his high-heeled riding boots all under a huge 'ten-gallon' hat. His initial surprise had gone at having a second visitor between the time he first saw my Rover and he joined us at the bush table for a mug of tea. He also had heard of my work already but couldn't understand what I was doing here, knowing his station track only led back to Walgun. Here it was virtually a dead end. It did go on east a little further to a windmill and tank and an old abandoned humpy named Talawana, but that was positively the last of anything whatsoever for well over 1000 kilometres to the east. I told him I knew that and this was the very reason I'd chosen his place to set off from on my expedition. He didn't like that at all and stated flatly that I'd die for sure out there in the Gibson Desert, but soon he could see he wasn't going to talk me out of it. He admitted he'd heard stories about me for many years and grudgingly conceded defeat.

Of course I'd camp there for the night and he wanted to know if there was anything I needed as a last chance for the trip. The sight of the box of salt reminded me that I had used nearly all I had on the way to Marble Bar and hadn't replaced it and some of that would be all I'd be able to carry apart from what I already had. He poured some into a jam tin and said 'This is the best they put up in Nullagine; it's Iodine salt'. I wasn't so sure about this until I read the label, 'The Finest Iodised Salt'.

After the mugs of tea and damper and treacle, we sat outside on the verandah while we discussed my trip. The screened-off portion of the windmill tower just outside the fence was the bathroom, the screening put up to stop the wind from blowing the water away into the dust while showering. I asked Bill how he came to own this area and where the name came from. The place was up for sale and as he went in to secure it they asked him what he was going to name it, showing him a map of the station with a dry creek bed running past called the Billanooka Creek. That settled that and with a few bullocks he took up occupancy, after building this homestead. This wasn't to be permanent of course, as he was putting up a proper house across the flat, bit by bit as he had time. We all walked over to inspect the progress which comprised a few posts set in concrete made of heavy bore casing and he went on to explain the design. 'This 'ere is the sittin' room' he announced as he stood on one area of dirt surrounded by four posts. I learned that he had four sons somewhere and wondered if they could come back to help him but he told me they wouldn't spare the time and said he wished he had four daughters instead. I couldn't see how they would be able to help in this sort of work until he explained his logic. 'If I had four daughters, each one would have a string of boy-friends, and that would give me dozens of willing helpers.'

Back on the other verandah he told me the deserted Talawana ruins had once been that station homestead, but a new owner moved a few kilometres further south to build and I wondered why the difference. 'He'll get a better view of the Robertson Range down there.' Colin Grant was the new owner who recently had made an extremely rare trip to Perth. Down there in new city boots, old corns on his toes began to hurt so he sat down on the footpath, removed the stiff leather, and with a penknife from his belt pouch he began paring down the thick knobs. A policeman soon appeared standing ominously over him in the crowd. About to run him in as a vagrant, the man from the force asked him where he came from and in Colin's words on getting back to the bush, 'The ignorant coot hadn't even heard of the Robertson Range.'

Between Billanooka and Talawana the abandoned remains of a rabbit-proof fence had to be crossed on the station track linking the two and this became the next topic as we talked to each other through the dangling stirrup straps and stockwhips. This had been also surveyed by Alfred Canning and although it was a tremendous feat in itself, he later was remembered only for his famous stock route. Traversing the fringes of the Great Victoria, Gibson, and Great Sandy deserts from south to north, it wound its way from the Great Australian Bight in the Southern Ocean near Esperance for almost 2000 kilometres to the southern end of the Eighty Mile Beach near Port Hedland on the Indian Ocean. The fence which was subsequently erected was an attempt by the Western Australian Government to prevent plagues of rabbits from the deserts over-running the cattle country. Milan Iskra had to cross over it near Jiggalong Mission on his trek to Ethel Creek although he might not have even been aware of it, for it had long since fallen into such disrepair that long sections were no longer in existence. As this fence passed within a few kilometres of Billanooka I was keen to see some trace of it on my way the next morning. At this point I would be about three-quarters along its length from the south.

After taking what I thought might be my last shower for a long time, under the windmill, we had some salt beef and damper for tea and were all asleep soon after. Bill was in the black interior of his shed, the old visitor on the verandah, and I took up my place as I had for the year so far in the back of my Land Rover.

Equally early next morning we were all up in the freezing cold of early August and after Bill's solemn handshake I had the impression that he was sure he'd be the last person to ever see me alive or any other way. I told him the next time I did call in it would be from the

other direction, complete with a graded road which would lead a traveller from his station clear through to Alice Springs.

I could still see the two of them standing on the dusty flat outside the wire fence around the hut, slowly shaking their heads as I drove into the light scrub beyond the clearing, complete with my tin of 'Iodine Salt'.

7
Discoveries in the Desert

After a few kilometres of driving on Colin's station track hidden completely in places by 2-metre high spinifex tops, I came to the bend which Bill has described as being near to the rabbit fence crossing. I slowed down to try and find some trace of it. Travelling already at almost a walking pace, the operation of slowing wasn't hard and soon a couple of posts appeared. I was elated to discover what must have been an original survey peg of Canning's party, a squared off thick bush wood affair still in place preserved from rot in this dry country. The bevel at the top was still in evidence although over the years some splintering had taken place. The type of wood he had chosen had also resisted white ants. The peg was alongside one of the fence posts 100 metres from the track, which I found by aligning two others still there and anything but vertical.

On this trip I had already planned to cut the stock route where it wound around to the north of Lake Disappointment at two of Canning's wells, numbers 23 and 24. Here I decided if possible to rediscover them and construct the road to pass right next to them, offering a possible meagre supply of water to any future traveller on my new road. If nothing else they would at least prove a great, if not only, point of interest on the long drag over the desert, as they were by rough plot right on my path anyway. They had been put there by the same man who had hammered in this peg around seventy years previously and the thoughts of that occupied me until I came to the windmill and stock tank at a down turn in the track to Talawana. The tank was brimful of good quality bore water and I knew we would be able to fill our truck tanks from it when we all arrived here months later with the road. I was still optimistic at the success of this last project even though a lot of work in exploring, surveying, and actually making had yet to be done. We had done it all so many times before but every stage presented its own set of huge problems which we met head on and dispensed with as they arose.

A stone's throw further on after leaving the dead tree by the side of the tank covered by thousands of finches, the ruins of old Talawana lay just inside the last post-and-wire fence between here and Alice Springs. The remains of an old fireplace, a few sheets of corrugated iron, and a couple of posts were all that was left and at first I couldn't be sure that this was really the site of the old homestead. Of course the new one lay a dozen or so kilometres further south but I would call in there another time to see it as the return 25 kilometres would be better used on the start of my expedition. I could see the Robertson Range further on in that direction and understood how the Perth policeman would not have known about it offhand. I thought he wouldn't be alone in his ignorance.

The area opposite the old ruins was an open ironstone gravel flat and I could already see it as a 'T' junction with our road from the east. It would also be easy to plot on updated maps as the position of old Talawana was already marked. As usual without any great fuss, I turned the Rover towards the east and drove across the gravel into the spinifex surrounding it leaving behind wheeltracks which would govern the final location of the road. These would last easily until the heavy grader left its much more permanent imprint.

There was another homestead further to the north-west, Balfour Downs, which I had seen marked months before when I had been planning this line of attack. Originally it seemed the best point to start but as Talawana was 30 kilometres further east and could still be reached by existing tracks which I didn't know about until the last few days, I reasoned that every little bit would help. Much

Top: The construction party's month-long camp when the grader broke down. *Bottom:* Doug Stoneham finds out first hand how to dismantle the broken gearbox under his grader

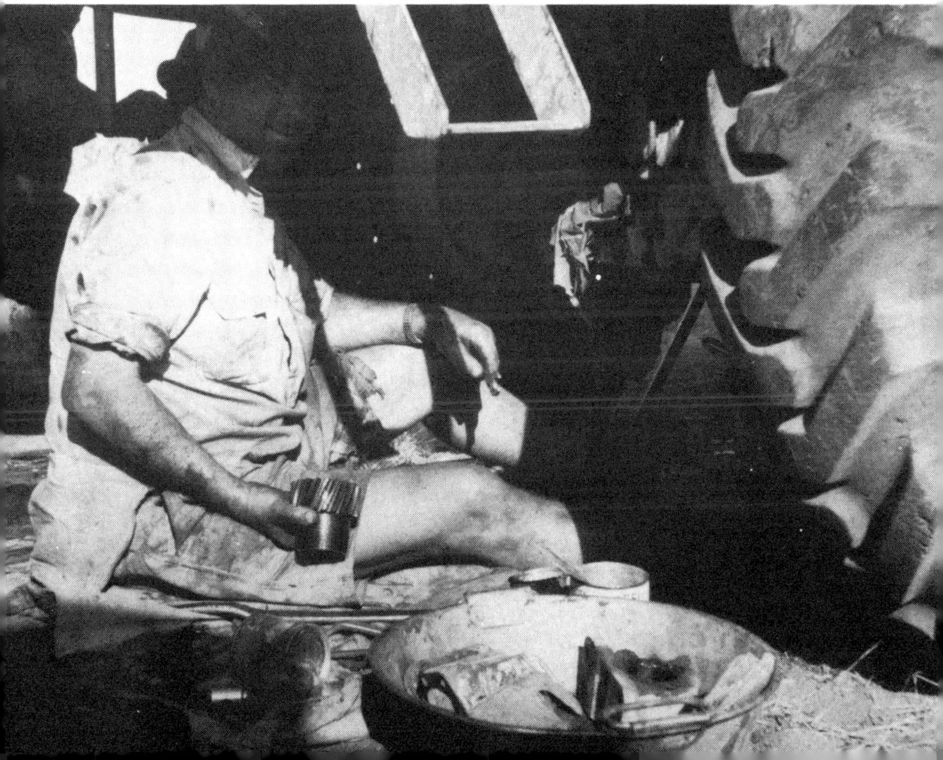

later I met the owner of Balfour Downs who turned out to be none other than William Holden, and I wondered if the 'other' one would have been flattered. A more grizzled-up, hard-as-nails bushman it would be quite impossible to find anywhere in the outback.

Although the familiar sandridges reared up in the first few kilometres, coming at them end on for once they presented no trouble at all and I soon fell into a very geometrical pattern for about 30 kilometres. As they loomed up I angled exactly south-east until approaching the next when the direction changed to due east. South-east, east, south-east, east, on and on it went and I wondered what this road would look like on a map when it was made. To reach the latitude of Well 23 and the Karara Soaks at the site of Well 24 on the Canning Stock Route, I had to drop about 25 kilometres southerly anyway, so it went well for me until reaching the 50-kilometre mark.

The whole nature of the country changed geologically after that for the next 100 kilometres. At the end of the 'geometrical' section the Poisonbush Range could be seen to the north, named after the deadly camel poison tree, and I steered between it and the Horse Track Range to the south. The intervening country presented 20 kilometres of the roughest rocky going to which anyone could subject a little Land Rover. It must have looked like a cork on the ocean as it bobbed up and down, in and out of the 50-centimetre deep holes in the limestone, and of course I wondered how the grader blade would handle it. There was no way around this belt which was hemmed in by the two ranges, and with the terrific flexing of the tyres I had to change two flats in the middle of it all. Jacking a vehicle up when it is already perched at an impossible angle is not easy but this went on out there continually. Admittedly sometimes harder than others, I hoped this wouldn't keep up too long as I doubted if I could ever reach the Gary Highway at all at this rate.

Within sight of the Wells Range also to the south, I felt the rocky stretch was relenting a little and reluctant to stop and camp before I cleared it, I carried on at a

Top: The crashed Cessna 175 discovered in the desert by (from left) Left Hand Jumbo, Inspector Bert Anderson, Shovel Shovel, Constable J. Graysmark, George Anderson. *Bottom:* Rex Flatman confronted with the results of Doug's bush mechanics, the contents of the grader gearbox.

pitifully slow pace until almost dark. Just as I thought that this would never end the sand took over, covered in huge spinifex tussocks, but I stopped there and then and with a feeling of elation camped in a small sandy clearing. There were two flat tyres to mend but I decided against observing the stars for my position because of the easy-to-plot beginnings of this trip. I had come about 70 kilometres since leaving Talawana, and hadn't eaten anything since Bill's damper and treacle. The extra 18 litres of petrol from the tin on the bonnet had long since gone into the tank and the empty tin discarded.

I discovered much later that my camp that night coincided almost exactly with the point where, in 1892, Surveyor Charles Wells made his change of course to rejoin his party from which he had split up 170 kilometres further to the east. At a place he named Separation Well they parted and while the others pushed off over 300 kilometres north to Joanna Spring, Wells headed west to the area of my camp that night and then altered his direction to the north-east also to Joanna Spring. He eventually died a terrible death alone in the desert there and his body was not found until 1897 by his uncle, Lawrence Wells, who took the remains to Adelaide, and the Wells Range, past which I had just driven over the rough limestone stretch, was named after him.

Yet another rocky outcrop labelled the Emu Range also to the south appeared the next day as I continued on towards the plotted position of the McKay Range, all over spinifex and sand country. One time the sandridges on either side of me met in front and I was forced to drive up and over them for the first crossing so far. I noted that in my diary and knew I'd be spending much time on reconnaissance on the way back to avoid this spot.

From my camp that night I knew I had to make up about 15 kilometres more south and at every opportunity veered to the right. I was pleased at only one more flat tyre that day to mend and still was not in need of an astrofix. I was now 170 kilometres on my way and no other mechanical trouble so far. I still did not know the excitement to come on this trip as I lay down early on the freezing ground in the open to sleep, after eating the contents of a tin of meat.

The next day I found myself in an impossible situation, completely barred from further onward movement. Driving slowly south past a large rocky jump-up, I saw a deep inlet into its depths to the east and steered into it. In about a kilometre, the sides of the ravine closed in with an accompanying solid wall of thicker growth of bushes through which I slowly forced the well-protected Rover. The fallen rocks became larger until the opening closed off altogether in a tangled mass of dead trees, bushes, and mountains of rock which defied any further progress, even with a bulldozer. At this stage I could neither turn around or even open the Rover's door against the heavy branches and conceding defeat, I was forced to reverse out of it a metre at a time. This took hours and used that much extra precious petrol for nothing gained. These were the instances for which much reserve fuel was always carried. I didn't mind that operation so much as wondering how I was going to clear this great obstacle, in the event of getting out of it in one piece in the first place. Eventually I was able to open the door to find a place open enough to turn around and I knew how grateful I had been to have avoided collecting a flat tyre at the head of this hopeless gorge.

Continuing in the only direction left open to me, I followed the wall of rock comprising, as I was to discover later, the western end of the McKay Range, until another inroad appeared into it. Not wanting a repeat performance I left the vehicle where it was and walked into it until I could see daylight ahead. This was several kilometres from the Rover and as the sun was sinking fast, I plodded back to it.

Before the blackness of the night closed in, I had pushed right through this opening and the daylight I saw ahead when on foot was there all right but only off into the sky as seen from the top of a miniature cliff. I could see after another hike that it would be possible to slide the Rover down the steep rocky slope and also that if I did there would definitely be no hope of going back. There was no other way through and not wanting to waste more petrol again retreating from this gully, there was nothing else for it but to attempt the descent and quickly before dark.

On the way down I only hoped the way would be clear ahead but it was already too dark to see far and after crossing a deep, dry waterway at the bottom, at a great risk of rolling the top-heavy vehicle, I camped again among the spinifex just clear of it all. Sleep doesn't usually come easily with the realisation that you might have worked your way into a corner from which there is no escape, but sheer tiredness came to the rescue. I would carry out an astrofix another night.

The situation early next morning hadn't improved at all, as I still could see no way out, for I was hemmed in by a high and very rocky circle of mountains. It was like being in a huge basin, so as usual in these cases I drove off in the direction I wanted to go as if there were no obstacles at all and would see what happened.

Over the millions of years, this natural watershed had directed any rain which had deigned to fall in this desolate area into one main channel, carving out a deep gash in the floor of the basin and I was soon lumbering along slowly on the southern rim. I was very relieved at the sight of this because the river bed might lead out of this enclosed arena to the open country once more.

Rounding a bend in its course I suddenly knew my present predicament was all over as I saw two things at once. Firstly the early morning sun glinting from a long pool of fresh water still there since some recent rain during the winter and best of all a definite opening between the circle of ranges with the familiar sandridges showing themselves in the distance beyond. I never thought I'd be pleased to see sandridges but here they spelled out very clearly my escape. The water in itself in this country was an unheard of discovery, crystal clear and a metre deep. Healthy white ghost gums lined the banks and after the going the day before, it was an absolute paradise of a place which I knew I would never forget. The reflections of the stately gums were mirrored in the perfectly still 80-metre long pool and although not short of water I did replenish the tank, after which an unexpected bath followed. I had thought Bill's windmill shower was to be my last for many weeks!

It wasn't long before signs of human life appeared in the shape of fresh bare footprints and newly broken sticks and although these were made by Aborigines I knew there would be no more remote tribe in Australia than these. Further positive evidence of their presence came as soon as I carried on, reluctantly leaving the water behind. Rising above the high spinifex tops and occasional mallee and mulga trees across the intervening open country to the first of the sandhills was a spiral of smoke. They were still here and also in the direction I had decided to go. With great excitement I closed the gap as quickly as the spinifex would allow but not before climbing out to take a last look at the rocky ranges which only hours before threatened to become my prison.

Clear of the burning tussocks I settled down to await a meeting I was sure would take place eventually, for I knew they would have been aware of my presence possibly even before I emerged from the basin. The sound of the engine would be picked up by their sharp hearing in this otherwise deathly quiet desert. While I was waiting I took an observation of the sun for latitude to fix this position and help with my onward direction towards Well 23, still

about 80 kilometres ahead. During this operation I actually saw some Aborigines through the theodolite telescope and knew a quiet wait was the only way I would ever make contact with them.

Finally after waiting until mid-afternoon, two wild-looking Aborigines stood up and strode over, jabbing their handfuls of spears into the sand on the way and a most historic meeting took place on the spot. I was to discover much more about this tribe later in the year after the road was through from some Ethel Creek Aborigines who came back out with us to interview them. Because of the absolute remoteness of this area I wondered at this time if they had ever had contact with our form of civilisation before, but right then I felt I should press on with my lone expedition as I had a long way over unknown country to go.

There was only time from where I left the Aborigines to struggle on 20 or so kilometres before dark and I camped once again among the spinifex. Knowing there was a reasonable chance of reaching the Canning Stock Route during the following day, I spent that night obtaining my exact location from the stars. The result would be doubly useful, not only to plot a more accurate direction to Well 23 to travel the next day but combined with the speedo reading and sun latitude at the meeting area, I could back plot a pin-point on the map where the meeting had taken place. I knew I would be seeing them again road or no road and their exact position would be needed.

Just 2 metres after trying to make a start next morning, the front tyre collapsed like a deflated balloon. A wooden stake must have been waiting patiently in front of the wheel all night and it had to be changed within reaching distance of my camp. Another day of spinifex bashing put the Rover and I alongside a salt lake and another astrofix told me that Well 23 should be about 10 kilometres to my north-east.

Again without anything to eat before heading off, I aimed the vehicle in that direction next morning early with mounting excitement in anticipation of discovering the well. The going was not easy with the rock outcrops and water-worn gutters in between but in a relatively short time I broke out on to a scrubby flat which extended many kilometres unbroken in all directions ahead. I worked out that the well should be another kilometre further on but wondered who would put a well down on a flat bush-strewn plain. Generally a little help is sought from local topography where infrequent rain would run off hills and seep into the dry ground quickly, gradually building up an underground supply.

In any case after pushing out on to the flat to the calculated position from the astrofix, I reobserved the sun for latitude at midday and this confirmed that I was very close to my goal. I stood on the Rover's roof scanning the full circle with binoculars round and round but not a sign of the whip pole showed itself, although I knew most of it would be hidden by the low scrub. I went back over to the foothills of the range from which I had just emerged to see if those were hiding the well, but still with no results.

Rather than remain in this area for another whole day in order to reobserve the stars that night, I decided I would push on to concentrate on finding Well 24 first. On our way back I would be able to make a more concerted effort to find this one with more food to hand in our truck than I had left then, but at least I knew within a kilometre the location of Well 23. Yet another astrofix that night would tell me the whole story but I resolved quite certainly not to continue on before finding the Karara Soak and also the well. This was going to govern the whole location of that section of the new road from the Gary Highway and it just had to be found.

I couldn't complete the calculations quickly enough by the light of the Rover that night after finishing the astrofix. This seemed to be a nightly ritual lately but the results were very rewarding. I was within a kilometre of Well 24.

Reasonably high mountain ranges were all around me and there was only one line I could take between them which was right on the calculated direction anyway from my camp that night. In due course next morning I stopped on a raised sandbar between the hills knowing that point must be within 500 metres from the well at the most.

Where could it be in this sort of place? Only 15 kilometres easterly from my estimated position for Well 23, it seemed equally as unlikely a place for a well but it was up to me to find it even though it was like looking for a needle in a haystack.

I hadn't eaten very much for the last few days, not wanting to use up the time in anything but the discovery of these sites and this surely wasn't the time to think of food either. Binoculars in hand I resumed my place on the roof of the Rover among the petrol drums, stirrup straps, and spare tyres and began a scan of my surrounds. After one slow complete circle without success I started another even slower revolution in the opposite direction. Just as I had almost finished, feeling more subdued by the minute, I saw it, the regular shape of a straight whip pole with its big iron pulley wheel on its top. This was nestling in hard against a rocky cliff face and I could even see the supporting posts and parts of the iron trough. It's impossible to describe the feeling of excitement and relief at a success such as this based on many astrofixes and sun observations and after hundreds of kilometres of hard travelling into trackless country. To actually discover something which occupies an area 2 metres square in hundreds of thousands of square kilometres of sandridges, says a lot for the careful fixing of these wells by Canning and Trotman.

In any event the position of the Karara Soak with its Well 24 would never be lost to me now and climbing down from the roof I drove off the sandridge and over to it. Apart from the whip pole, rusted troughs, and jinny wheel posts, the first thing I found was a huge bush wooden dish made and used by Aborigines to carry their piccaninnies. Water was often put into these dishes, plus some spinifex tops to stop it splashing out, although this one had been there for some time and was probably left by the tribe I had encountered days before. The well was still neatly timbered and about 4 metres deep, half full of reddish putrid water some of which I pulled up in a billy on a string to taste. Any future traveller would at least have some liquid to pour over himself if not to replenish his drinking water tank.

As I walked around searching for any other artefact which might be lying about, I could never have guessed in my wildest imagination that this and the road which was to follow, would be a feature in a film later made out here for people to see back in the cities. Author Hammond Innes somehow heard about the road less than a decade after we had finished making it and wrote a book, later made into a film, leading up to a fabulous fortune of copper hidden out here in the desert. The only access to this fictitious 'McIlroy's Monster' was our road passing by the Karara Soak at Well 24. He named his story *The Golden Soak*. I have seen it long since on television, sitting in the comfort of a big chair, and it certainly brought back vivid memories of this eventful discovery on this special day in the desert. No other viewer on earth could have looked at it with the same feeling as I had, remembering all that led up to this moment. Although Hammond Innes described our road as a rough survey track which it probably was when he saw it, I thought he might have preferred it such as it was to none at all, as was the case right here and now. He didn't have to observe a string of astrofixes to find Karara Soak either, so at least navigation wasn't a problem for him.

I also was not to know that fifteen years later, my own family would be pouring water over themselves pulled up in a bucket from Well 24 to serve as our first bath since leaving Adelaide on a long 'holiday' trip over our roads. First you make your roads, then you can take your family on a trip! The day of that community bath coincided with my wife's birthday and she mentioned she would have liked the number of the well to have equalled her age.

All this was to be in the future but right then I couldn't use any more time lingering at this spot and I drove off to attempt to clear the rock cliff and continue on towards the Gary Highway, still 200 kilometres somewhere ahead.

In any case I had to press on and so help Hammond Innes whose imaginary 'monster' was to lie yet further east among the sandhills in the desert, near the road yet to be made.

8
Windy Corner

The rock cliff petered out to ground level in a kilometre or so to the north, allowing me to turn off the natural course of the stock route and resume my easterly direction. I had been on the line of the former cattle drives since the vicinity of Well 23 and I knew its north-easterly trend would lead on to cut our latest road to Callawa at Well 35. The only evidence of the stock route I had found in this area so far, apart from Well 24, was a weathered piece of horn from one of the beasts which was enough to reassure me I was on the original trail. Nothing else whatsoever gave evidence of its presence and if it had not been for the stars, I would never have known of its existence in this locality.

Soon after rounding the northern end of the cliff, the first of a long series of salt lakes showed itself and even after I walked ahead to test the surface, I nearly got the Rover bogged over one short crossing. As I climbed up the bank on the far side I knew that would not happen again and that I would later find another crossing for the grader. To become bogged in a salt lake in this country alone and hundreds of trackless kilometres to anywhere was the last thing I could afford to do, so I proceeded with much more caution and camped another few kilometres further on. I needed full daylight ahead to weave through this maze of salt pans. Another flat tyre had to be mended before lying down on my canvas sheet in a particularly rough area, not daring to move further as dusk closed in.

This was the very place where two months later to the

day the gearbox in this same Rover began its break-up, forcing a nightmare drive of 700 kilometres to Warburton Mission alone using only top gear. That was after the road had progressed past this point and I remembered being glad that the same trouble hadn't happened on this occasion. If it had and with no road out either way for so great a distance, it could well have been the end of everything including myself.

A large salt lake developed on the northern side of my course and a long high sandridge paralleled it to the south leaving a narrow ledge in between. I was forced to carry on along it for at least a kilometre over high wind-blown hummocks of spinifex and samphire at much less than a walking pace. I thought months later this same stretch could easily have also contributed to the downfall of the grader gearbox as it wrestled with it to carve out a smooth access track. As I noted in my diary that day, this was a very rough area with dozens of 'bad spots'.

Worse was yet to come at the far end of the salt lake when the high sandridge curved around in front of me to stop at the salt surface. Across a narrow neck another high sandridge began where the other left off and I just had to cross over to it with again no other way around. Walking over it this time with a shovel I was quite pleased to see that the holes I dug didn't develop into salty, bottomless, blue mud as is normally the case. The very reason for the narrowness of this neck was explained by the relative solidness of the underlying layer, so reluctant as I was to venture out on to it, I knew I had to anyway. Making it at speed to the far bank I still wondered if it would support the many more tonnes of the grader later on.

That proved to be the last of the troubles I had to overcome for the rest of the expedition. I would have been much more contented in my mind had I known but as I pushed on the salt lakes fell behind to be replaced by wide spinifex valleys between the parallel sandridges. These were aiming in the exact E.S.E. direction in which I wanted to go and the kilometres passed at an easy, if not fast rate, the high tussocks reducing any progress to the usual walking pace.

This direction would veer me towards the Tropic of Capricorn 40 kilometres to the south, which cut the Gary at a point along its length where I planned to establish the junction. No astrofixes were needed that night or for the next 100 kilometres because I couldn't stray to the left or right even if I had wanted to. By the hour as I drove I felt the worst was behind me and more so when at the end of 100 kilometres even the sandhills stopped abruptly and the whole country ahead reverted to open spinifex prairies, dotted by solid clumps of mulgas which were easy to bypass.

The carefully compensated, oil-bath aircraft compass installed over the steering wheel was all I needed from then on. No more standing up to a theodolite in the freezing nights reading angles on to stars between mending flat tyres and the subsequent calculations by battery light afterwards. These would always have to be done before collapsing in my swag that same night to tell me what direction I must take next morning, and I often fell asleep periodically doing them. My clear course was now true east until I cut the Gary Highway as I had finally reached the latitude of Capricorn.

Although bitingly cold throughout that expedition in early August, the days had been perfect in spite of the never-ending humps of spinifex over which I had to travel at a snail's pace for weeks. This had left me in such a condition each night as to not be able to appreciate them. Then came the historic day with my eyes set on a far-off patch of scrub barely visible in the distance and I was resigned to struggle across to it from the previous clump as I trundled the Rover along the depression separating it from me, when my battered state of mind suddenly turned to elation. Unexpectedly I had landed on the Gary Highway and was half-way across it before I realised it, concentrating as I was on the far horizon. The expedition had abruptly come to an end in the space of a second. I had been observing stars and obtaining latitude readings from the sun throughout the trip and knew to a pencil point where I was at all times on my blank map and the same had been the case when making the Gary Highway, so the word 'unexpectedly' perhaps wasn't really correct. It only seemed to be that way after weeks of crawling easterly towards my goal and that I had been set for another long stretch ahead when that destination suddenly cut across my path. For days I thought I would never reach it with the relatively few kilometres a day I could move, but all the time I really knew it had to come.

As soon as the reality of it had penetrated I switched off the engine and climbed very stiffly out on to the smooth graded surface free of those dreaded skylines of rough spinifex. Actually I knew them to be much more preferable to other horizons of mulga scrub and sandhills and I had been glad to confirm the earlier plan of handling this section with the grader on its own, but right then and there I couldn't fully appreciate my good fortune—only the fact that several seconds before I had been on an expedition and now it was over.

To experience the indescribable sensation of the ultimate success of any project big or small, a person has to put himself through a great ordeal either mentally or physically, and the tougher the ordeal the greater the feeling of elation when it's over. When I had finally crawled over the leading windrow of the Gary Highway I knew I could not hope to relate to anyone the complete feeling of relief I had, as the doubts as to whether I could make it over the past weeks fell away immediately. I had traversed over 500 kilometres of unknown desert apart from the brief crossing over the Canning Stock Route and I knew I could, with several variations in the middle, make a graded road back along the course of my wheeltracks.

It had been about the locality of this junction, I remembered, when we had been making that north-south road, how we were forced to camp for several days in the one spot after two short but heavy deluges of rain which caused the surface to become apparently bottomless. The exact distance from the Gunbarrel Highway was still recorded in my little diary and as I recalled the very camp where it had taken place I then decided to obtain a vehicle speedo reading to it from that future corner. That would supply the number of kilometres north and south to the other two main access roads. Not really being sure if that rain camp was to the right or left, I made a calculated guess that it should be to the north, so clambering back into the cabin, I drove up on the only road I had seen for weeks, and tried to locate it. In any case it was a novelty to move along in an even horizontal line instead of the usual bone shattering up and down motion.

The speedometer reading at the 'highway' showed I had come over 500 kilometres across unknown country from Talawana, making it certainly the first pilgrimage that had ever been made over this area by anything, let alone a motor vehicle. I had emptied all the petrol drums carried separately on the roof, the few tins tied on to the bonnet as a last resort, and also the spare tank built into the vehicle at our Salisbury workshops. Not daring to test the level in the one remaining standard tank after turning the last tap, I tried it before setting off in search of the rain camp. There was barely 20 litres left of the 400 I had started out with. One or more less of the spare tins tied on at the last minute would have stranded me out on the plains and a vastly different chapter in the history of the opening up of that section would have resulted.

As I drove, the endless false horizons kept coming and going and just as I began to wonder if the old camp site might have been south of the future corner instead, I recognised the rise it had been on out of the boggy intervening depressions. The distance to it was 14 kilometres and as this camp had been 210 kilometres from the Gunbarrel Highway, then the junction I had just made would stand at a distance of 196 kilometres. According also to my diary, the whole length of the Gary Highway was 340 kilometres and now I had enough information to print on the sign which I intended to make for the corner. The intersection at the northern end of the 'highway' which I had named Gary Junction would then be 144 kilometres away.

Back at the new wheeltracks I had just made, I again checked the amount of fuel remaining and determined that I would have to settle down there until the rest of my camp appeared. I had arranged with them a month before, when I had last seen them at Port Hedland on the Indian Ocean, for them to return along the road we had just constructed over the Great Sandy Desert back to Gary Junction, then travel south along Gary Highway until they met up with me. Assuming of course that I had been successful in negotiating those hundreds of kilometres of desert, I would camp wherever I came out until they arrived. That also depended on their completing the 1100 kilometres back with no major breakdowns, but as the party had several vehicles somebody should be able to get through.

The reason that I had decided to originate this expedition from its western end stemmed from from the contact we had with the nature of the sandridges on the north-west road. Many of the long drawn-out dunes seemed to converge upon their neighbours at the western ends of the valleys, leaving all their trailing ends pointing to the east. Consequently as I probed ahead on the Great Sandy Desert road I found I was forever being blocked off ahead where two adjoining ridges met and this involved many hundreds of kilometres of wasted reconnaissance. Since I had so often been forced to retreat and try another 'groove', I had the impression that if we had been coming from the west, we could have carried on almost indefinitely in whichever valley we happened to be in. It was rather like attacking a table fork from the prong end compared with starting from the handle.

I positioned the Rover just off the road, oriented in a direction where I could easily see the dust of any approaching vehicle from the north, climbed out of the cabin for the last time, and settled down for an enforced wait of a completely unknown duration. Sometimes in the days or weeks ahead, the Gunbarrel Boys might appear over the northern undulation with or without the full complement of our team. Two trucks, one towing a water cart and the other a trailer with black and battered cooking gear on board in turn shackled to a small refrigerator trailer, a workshop Land Rover, and a Caterpillar road grader, made up the expected convoy and it was reasonable to assume somebody might arrive.

Thinking of the water trailer and ration truck made me remember how little of both these items I still had left after the long trip. It was still very cold with almost freezing nights and this had contributed to the fact that I still had a little water left as the radiator did not need constant filling in those temperatures, but the food was almost all gone. Not that I had started off with very much and had used what there was sparingly, but on the other hand each small article of food I did eat meant the last of that particular commodity. The satisfaction of surviving the expedition and being once more on a made road far outweighed any problem the shortage of food could bring and I barely gave that a second thought.

The very first job I planned for myself was to observe the stars that night for an accurate latitude and longitude fix for this junction. This would be forwarded with all the others to the headquarters of the National Mapping Council for the future compilations of new maps which were constantly being brought out as our work made inroads into this previously unmapped wilderness. The results would also be stamped on to my aluminium sign plate which was the second operation I would be doing, and this would then be erected there for the use of any future traveller including the mapping teams. One way and another I would be kept busy for several days including a day's calculation of the astrofix.

My present Land Rover had been converted to make it possible for me to sleep in it for once out of the elements and I had soon reason to silently thank the boys at our workshops who had carried out my designs. I could also sit inside with the calculation books spread out on a board carried under my swag, without the need of weighing down the pages with stones or tools against the winds. Sometimes it had been still necessary to roll out the swag on the ground but with the much lightened load I was glad to be able to escape from the cold during this waiting period. It soon was to become clear that it was not only from the cold that the Rover offered protection.

On this area so devoid of scrub, firewood was quite scarce but as I didn't have anything to cook it would not

Jackie, the author's eleven-year-old daughter, finally gets to see 'her' junction on the Gunbarrel Highway

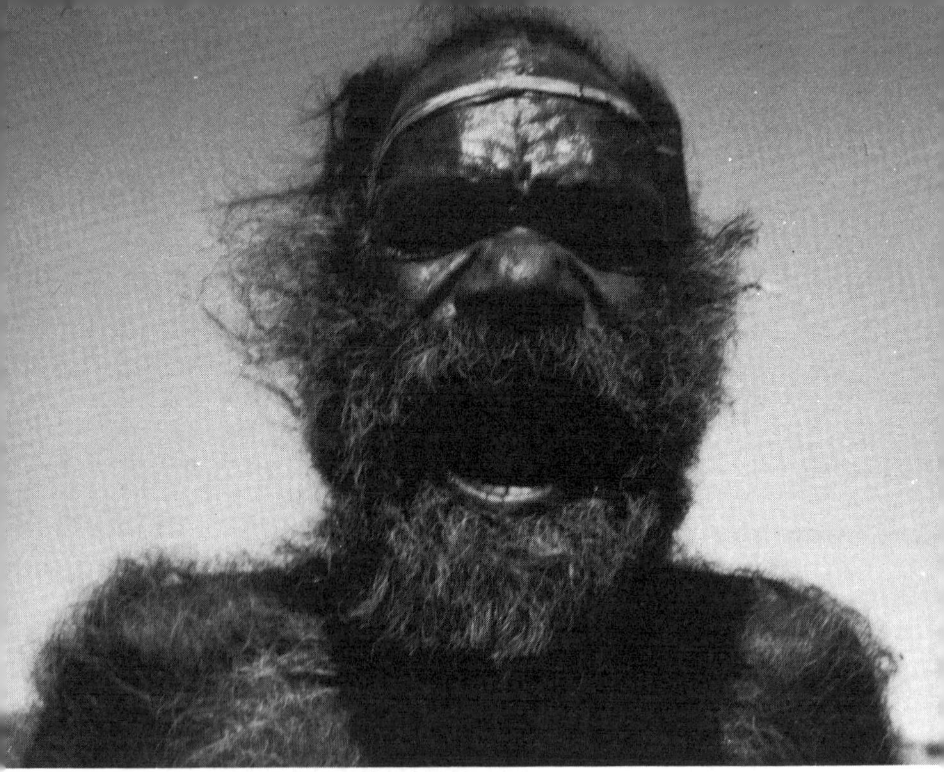

present any loss. Only a little warmth at nights might be welcomed, but my swag could take care of that.

Throughout that first night I recorded readings of stars observed and when I finally packed away my theodolite and books I had enough for a first-class position of where I was on the surface of the earth. My fingers had been completely without feeling as I pulled the blankets over me and it wasn't until well after sun-up that I woke, anxious to get on with the mounds of sums waiting in the field books. Late afternoon not only brought the final results with it but the growing feeling that there was a breeze moving the spinifex tops about with increasing vigour.

The value of this as yet unnamed junction told me I was camped on latitude south 23° 34′ 26″ and east longitude of 125° 11′ 32″, and these were the figures which would appear on my sign plate. They would also ultimately be processed in Melbourne to plot this position on the latest maps everywhere.

After venturing to open a small tin of meat for the day's meal, I had another sound sleep and with the arrival of the dawn, the breeze had turned into a definite wind. I quickly had the steel jack plate out on the plain with the aluminium placed on it and began lettering the sign for the junction which I hoped would be vital to later users of these roads.

As I hammered the alphabet steel punches, I felt the sand blowing against my ragged shirt and I was glad to complete my artwork and retreat into the back of the vehicle and wipe the mixture of sand and dust from my eyes. The microscopic fire I had made from a few sticks lying about had barely heated a tin of meat before the increasing wind scattered the last of the white ash and as the tepid contents of the tin disappeared while huddled in the Rover, the gusts had reached proportions that rocked it on it springs. The cabin doors and windows were shut tight as was the tailboard and door, and the particles of debris hurled along rained on the outer skin of the cubicle with ever increasing force as the volume of the accompanying noise rose.

Top: Hairy Lolly laughs heartily at his joke after grabbing author's toe during the writing of *Too Long in the Bush. Bottom:* Author's family has exciting reunion with Lolly fourteen years later. From left: author, Connie Sue, Lolly, Jackie, Gary, and wife Anne

Within the next hour I thought that the vehicle could almost be blown over on its side as it swayed from side to side when extra strong bursts assailed it and the atmosphere outside was fast becoming like night. The sand and dust storm was really under way when the sun became dulled and then almost blanked out altogether and a dark gloom appeared through the glass windscreen. The feeling of gratitude at being able to have this shelter from it was indiscribable and I also regarded it as fortunate that I had completed the astrofix before the country went berserk. Nothing whatsoever could be seen out of any of the windows and as the fury of the rampage soared, the temperature dropped in proportion until my little haven seemed as if packed in ice. All I could think of was losing myself in my swag with the canvas pulled over everything and waiting for it to abate.

I was still crouching in the back of the Rover *five days* later as the violence continued unchecked day after day. If it hadn't been for my watch I wouldn't have known if it were night time or day, not that it mattered in the least anyway. Very occasionally I gouged out the contents of the last of the tins of meat to ease the pangs of hunger which were becoming easier to put up with as the time went on. The early feelings of extreme hunger gradually pass as the system becomes accustomed to the lack of food but other visual results become apparent, when such things as knuckle bones protrude more than usual.

Although I had no immediate hope of posting it, during the wait I wrote a letter to George and Terry Anderson while the events of the expedition were still so fresh in my mind. I told them how Bill Ellery had given me some 'Iodine' salt and how he thought I was going too far out into the desert and how I agreed it was safer to stay close to the suburbs like Billanooka. I went on to tell them about the percentage of the Aboriginal men in the tribe I had discovered who only had one eye, wondering if some unknown ritual had been the cause. Also how those Aborigines had only burst out laughing after I told them I had just heard over the radio that a Dr Stephen Ward had died from an overdose of drugs. I did not forget to include the fact that George's concern for the petrol I carried went a long way to the success of the expedition.

It was during this prolonged confinement that a name presented itself to me for this main future road junction and long before the area had returned to sanity I was quite decided on what it would be called. The very obvious title of 'Windy Corner' kept repeating itself in my mind and when calmness at last settled on the scene, I replaced the aluminium plate on my 'anvil' and stamped out the new name boldly across the top. The new maps appeared years later, and I forever relive those five days as I read the printed place name of 'Windy Corner' at the turn-off.

9
Bush Mechanics

It had only been a couple of days after the wind had blown itself out that the rest of the party finally appeared over the rise to the north, all intact amid volumes of accompanying bull dust, and they lumbered across the flat to where I was waiting. The noise of the big diesel motor and clanging of the ration truck with its trailer first heralded their approach and as I looked out of the Rover in which I still huddled out of the cold, their dust was the first visible proof that they were actually here. I climbed out over the tail board and bustled about lighting the small fire I'd prepared with wood carried from a long way off as my visitors could probably do with a hot drink—provided they supplied the water, tea, and sugar. My rations by then were almost non-existent. We hadn't seen or had contact with each other since separating near the Indian Ocean and it was going to be an exciting reunion.

After their dust settled we all decided that it was no use camping on the corner completely devoid of firewood and after that one billy had been boiled and a slab of Paul's bread devoured under a mound of bully beef soaked with tomato sauce, we moved west to the first clump of mulga. Not however, before making the initial few hundred metres of our new road back along my tracks leading over that desolate country to Talawana, completely uninhabited except for that remote tribe of Aborigines west of the Canning Stock Route.

The party had come down our latest road hundreds upon hundreds of kilometres and our timing had proved remarkably accurate. With all that had taken place since we parted up near Marble Bar, for both of us to reach the same spot within a week or so of each other was nothing short of a miracle, although after all that was what was supposed to have happened.

When we positioned the grader on the Gary Highway at right angles pointing west, I retraced my expedition tracks to the previous patch of scrub and flashed a mirror signal for them to make the first cut. It was at least a start and on the second run the junction was opened out to enable the rest of our vehicles to round the corner and drive over the new surface to where an unlimited supply of wood lay waiting. What a change it would be to be able to stand around a large warm camp fire with plenty of food to eat after so long without either.

The grader on its arrival had a set of clutch plates which barely pulled it along the ground. The old trouble we had on the way to Callawa had worsened and it was only by a stroke of good fortune for us all that it held out at all on their way back, slipping and smoking as it was. They had attempted to regrade what we had done on the initial road but as the clutch gave out it was only the newly graded surface ahead which made it possible to move at all. In any event it did reach me under its own power but it was very apparent that a major operation would have to be done on it before we could attempt making the road to Talawana with it. At least there was enough left in it to grade that small beginning of the new road to the west, and I was able to install the new aluminium sign plate I had made at Windy Corner. This could be done while the others prepared their vehicles for the long trip back to the Giles Meteorological Station where the large-scale mechanical work on the grader could be carried out, a haul of 700 kilometres.

We only travelled about 100 kilometres on the way south to the Gunbarrel Highway when the clutch plates gave up altogether. No amount of coaxing from them would budge the heavy machine so it would be a towing job from there on right to Giles by the 3-tonne ration truck. It had been pulling the trailers of cooking apparatus and these were distributed to the workshop Rover and mine, and we were forced to continue on at a much reduced rate.

I had another sign plate made for the intersection of the Gary and Gunbarrel Highways so we all camped there to leave me time to erect it. It was to be of the same design as that at Windy Corner with an upraised flap from the top of a diesel drum and the rectangular shape of the flap had to be cut as usual with a hammer and chisel and the aluminium sheet bolted to the raised surface through holes once again drilled with my revolver.

We dragged ourselves into Giles three days later where I arranged over their powerful transmitter for our old friend Rex Flatman to be flown up with all the parts needed and carry out the repairs. Rex had been with us as a very efficient heavy equipment fitter and mechanic for years and knew this grader inside and out. Next day up came a Bristol Freighter to land on the airstrip which had been made with this same grader, bringing Rex with his new clutch plates and flywheel. The job of taking that huge engine out began immediately and we all helped while Rex did the job and directed. A great piping gantry had first to be erected over the grader to which was attached an endless chain hoist, before dozens of fuel and oil lines and levers could be disconnected. This would have been a sizeable job in a well-equipped workshop but here it was going to be done out in the open sun with makeshift help.

This looked like being quite a session and as our son Gary, of the now well-used Gary Highway fame, above all things at this time was due to be christened, I decided to fly all the way back to Adelaide on the Bristol's return trip for the event. This was carried out by Reverend Howell Witt, an old Woomera friend who later was to become Bishop of the whole north-west of Western Australia, including such areas as Ethel Creek.

A week or so later saw me back at Giles flying back via Maralinga and it took me two days to recover from the long hot bumpy ride. The grader was now as good as new, at least in its clutch department, after about 30 000 kilometres of grading behind it during the previous eight years with us in that country.

A day later and we were on our way back to Windy Corner to attack the road to Talawana, as yet marked only by my lonely set of wheeltracks just laid down a few weeks before. Before we set off there was an intense conference at Giles with a professor of anthropology who desperately wanted to meet and study the new tribe near the McKay Range. It seemed that the story of the discovery had spread very fast. Dr Donald Thompson held the chair in anthropology at the University of Melbourne, but he couldn't spare the time to wait for us to make the road. He was to arrange for me to take him out to meet them two years later.

Driving back along the Gunbarrel Highway to reach Jackie Junction took us only two days, with the grader once again travelling under its own power. We now also had a change of operators to drive it with the return of Doug Stoneham, who had been with us for the first six years as the bulldozer driver. He had been away for a year's spell to be with his wife and new daughter but agreed to come back for this last project. The grader he was driving now was travelling over roads that he himself had bulldozed years before.

The morning after the camp near Jackie Junction was quite a memorable one as far as I was concerned, as it was then I began writing the manuscript of a book to be later published under the title *Too Long in the Bush*. The recent trip to Adelaide had given me the final incentive to start it after an interview with the publishers.

Not long after our little cavalcade passed by the first of the new sign plates on the Gary Highway, the Jeep trailer towbar broke up, and this meant a repair job with the welding gear. To make the most use of the return trip, we decided to regrade sections of the 'highway'.

Being well into September the days were becoming quite hot, but the cold morning winds of this time of the year kept the flies at bay if nothing else. The strong dusty winds were upon us for days and we were always pleased to have the months immediately following winter behind us. As we mended a flat tyre on the grader just as we reached Windy Corner, Doug, who hadn't as yet seen it, remarked on the suitable name for 'this joint'.

At last, after all the interruptions of the major repair to the grader, the christening, and the anthropological conference, not to mention the long 700-kilometre return trip from Giles, we were ready to start again. Now we could actually launch into what was to become the last project ever to be carried out as a team by my old Gunbarrel Road Construction Party. We had already made the first couple of hundred metres before the interruptions with the then crippled grader, but now there was nothing else holding us up from completing the road from Windy Corner to Talawana.

At every opportunity as we worked towards the area of the salt lakes, where I would need to do a good deal of further reconnaissance, I added pages and then chapters to the story of surveying and making the Gunbarrel Highway. My plan was to put as much down in this desert setting as I could, not knowing that I would be able to actually type four chapters at Warburton, as a result of the grader breakdown in only a week's time.

As it turned out, the narrow crossing over the neck of the big salt lake did easily support the weight of the grader and the road progressed to the maze of smaller ones just short of Well 24. With time, food, and water to spare I discovered a safe path through these much easier than it seemed when I was on my own, and it wasn't long before the grader was on the sandy rise alongside the Karara Soak. We decided to grade a small offshoot the few hundred metres over to the well itself, and I thought how out of place the huge yellow machine looked as it turned around near the rusty trough. If only Alf Canning could have been there on that day to see it. He could never have imagined that anything like this could happen over half a century after his party laboriously dug out that well, and it was not only him I was thinking about. I myself couldn't yet accept the fact that we actually now had made a road linking this spot clear back to the Central Australian road system.

Positioning the grader on the route of the main road back on the sand rise, I arranged for the rest of the small party to come forward to view this most interesting feature but I suspected the history behind it all was lost completely on them. Paul looked at and said it was 'nice'. Grading on a kilometre to a good site for a camp I planned to leave the party there to service the vehicles and rest up while I went off to make a fine toothcomb search for Well 23.

Driving back along my wheeltracks for the 15 kilometres between these two wells, I again stopped on that scrubby plain which I knew must hold the secret and again climbed to the roof. I had come prepared to camp in that area for as long as it took to find it but no sooner had I began the same binocular search, the top 30 centimetres of a whip pole came into my field of view. There was barely enough of it to hold the pulley wheel showing above the scrub and it all happened within seconds of the beginning of the search. It must have passed the lens weeks before as I was again in the same spot as I had been on that expedition but it had been mid-afternoon and this was mid-morning. The angle of the sun showed it up against a different coloured background making it immediately visible, and I thought how its discovery would have brought on the same elation on the first trip as had Well 24.

Driving the few hundred metres over to it through the scrub, I had no less a feeling of excitement as I broke out on to a small open area with the well, whip pole, and rusty trough as its centre. That position would also never elude me again and as usual found it was about 4 metres deep, timbered, and half full of equally putrid water. It could be handy at a pinch for the constant boiling radiators we or anyone else for that matter experienced with the approaching summer. In this case we could construct the road easily within a metre of it and again I thought of Canning and the subsequent cattle drives. The drovers, if they hadn't stopped using the stock route, could have hearded the cattle along a graded road between Wells 23 and 24, a road which would surely come into existence on the following day.

The party was surprised to see me that same afternoon

as I drove in, for they had not expected my return for days after I had told them I was setting off on a long search. Everything seemed so much easier than it had been when I was there before, so many hundreds of kilometres away from anything, and when the road was established within touching distance of the whip pole, Paul again assured us he thought this too was 'nice'.

Four days later and just as I thought everything was almost leaping ahead, the gearbox on the grader decided to break up into little pieces and the whole project halted abruptly. Within 160 kilometres of Talawana and right at the place I had discovered the remotest tribe I was ever to find, the tired old grader had finally given up.

I had managed the steeply banked dry creek crossing with my Rover and was positioned on the wheel tracks I had made a few months before on the far side to guide the grader over to the western bank. Doug drove slowly down the bank to make a first tentative cut with the blade and then crossed the lowest part of the ditch to begin the upward slope. All was going well as he made the flat ground near my Rover and turned to open out the cut, with each subsequent crossing becoming easier. He again turned the giant machine for a third attack and aimed it back down the steep cutting. He was almost to the bottom when a decidedly expensive clatter momentarily drowned out everything else and stopped the grader dead where it was. The rear tandem wheels were hardly over the crest on their downward track and the front ones had come to rest on the floor of the miniature canyon. It sounded like a gigantic bag of nuts being ground to pulp with a loud metallic clanging. Doug suddenly closed the fuel lever and the big motor quickly died. We both knew what had happened and that this was surely going to break the routine of our day-to-day road making.

A tooth must have broken off a wheel in the gearbox and was instantly churned around by the others, crunching off more as it went. We had lived with such things as this for so long that we hardly mentioned it as I regained the other bank with the Rover using the partly made crossing. Doug climbed in and we drove back to the temporary camp informing our old cook Paul that the camp would now become permanent for an as yet unknown period. Before settling in we uncoupled his ration truck from the little fridge trailer, summoned Eric with the fuel supply waggon, and adding Quinny's long-distance supply truck to the convoy, we all drove the several hundred metres along the brand new road to the crippled grader.

For once on this work I didn't have the services of our usual heavy equipment fitter, who had been with our camp for years tending the heavy machinery as we pushed ever further out into the desert. Rex was at present almost 2000 kilometres by road away at our old atomic bomb site at Maralinga on the Nullarbor Plain and as his family had been missing him we thought he might have a spell down there. Without the bulldozer, the others could attend to the needs of the grader in normal maintenance, leaving Rex to periodically visit his home using the aircraft which regularly called at Maralinga. But this was something else again.

With the trucks all joined to each other by heavy steel cables and with my Rover waving about in front, we attached another cable to the grader down the bank and gradually took the strain. Amazingly the great yellow bulk moved backwards up the ramp and clear on to the level ground, after which any one of our vehicles could manoeuvre it over to the camp. Paul took his truck back to settle it in place for a long wait, while Quinny left Eric to drag it back on his own. I returned to the camp and guided them to a suitable spot free from the bulk of the spinifex where we could work on it. Our idea was to endeavour to dismantle the affected part after a conversation over my transceiver to Rex at Maralinga and then describe to him what we found to be wrong. He would be able to gather all the new replacement parts from the well-stocked workshops there and come out on a west-bound train on the Indian–Pacific railway to Rawlinna where I would meet him. After a 1400-kilometre drive entirely over our own roads, I would turn around and bring him plus the parts back out to the camp. He would reassemble it, after which operation I planned to return him to Rawlinna and the train for his journey back east to Maralinga. Once I deposited him on the train, I would return to Lake Disappointment and carry on with the road as if nothing had happened.

The fact that this operation would probably take many weeks didn't deter us in the least, as this sort of thing had been routine for so long. It would involve almost 6000 kilometres of travelling with weeks of camping on the way during which nothing more could be done on our project. An enforced spell from the constant ritual of shifting camp daily to the head of the road and the physical labours of keeping everything moving wouldn't go astray, and we would all be eager to resume at the end of it.

That plan had evolved in my mind and everything seemed to be quite straightforward as a means of coping with this present breakdown. There was admittedly a lot to do but when such a thing happens in the most remote country in Australia, large-scale measures are needed to handle it.

With the grader neatly positioned alongside the camp we set about clearing the spinifex clumps from around the open-air workshop with our shovels. Quinny with his usual bush humour asked us why we didn't smooth it all off first with the grader. The weather at the time was perfect although we had recently experienced the consistent high winds and sand storms which always assailed our little party in September. Now it was October and the heat was just beginning but the full impact of the approaching summer inferno was yet to hit us. At least we had that in our favour, we thought as the job was begun.

With canvas sheets on the sand to prevent the tools and parts from being lost, Doug settled himself under his grader and started unscrewing everything in sight attached to the gearbox. I erected the transceiver aerial and contacted the operator at Maralinga, asking for Rex to be summoned over to his microphone. It was amazing to be able to speak over such a vast distance from a little battery operated instrument, although now it is being done constantly. Somehow down in the cities crowded with complicated apparatus, the fact that people can talk to each other across the world in seconds doesn't seem to be anything unusual. Out here in the desert with nothing between us and the base station but sandhills, the wonder of it all never failed to impress us. Even experienced scientists with whom I'd camped away from their established laboratories, always remarked how wondrous it was when contacting our base network using radio devices which some of the older ones had even helped to develop themselves.

Within minutes Rex's voice came back to inform us that he was ready to listen to our latest troubles. He would help the situation with his technical knowledge, having been out with us in the same predicament so often himself.

To merely take a gearbox out of a grader and dismantle it sounds a straightforward sort of a thing to do but when it comes to actually trying, it is another story altogether. Some of the bolts and connections seem to defy attempts to be separated from it and one such occasion arose as I was talking to Rex. Doug came over covered in grease and declared that it was a physical impossibility to remove several parts without an oxy-acetylene torch. Describing the details over the microphone, instructions came back as to a special sequence that must be followed and after which it would literally fall off.

After two days spent under the machine, the whole contents of the box was spread out and the broken parts measured and described to Rex, who then knew what to bring. I told him to wait for another radio message from me which I would transmit when I neared Rawlinna and then come out on the next west-bound train. I could camp on the Nullarbor Plain by the siding until he arrived.

Being right on the spot of my earlier discovery of what I concluded must have been the most remote tribe of Aborigines in Australia, we received daily visits from several of them during all this activity. They were firm friends by this and although they would not stay long and remained a little distance from the camp, they always came at almost the exact time each day. It was uncanny the way they would appear at 3.40 p.m. in the afternoons and leave at 4 p.m. It didn't occur to me to think about their punctuality until one afternoon I saw Paul anxiously looking out across the desert while perpetually consulting his watch. I went to him jokingly asking him if he was expecting anyone and he looked quite worried as he replied that he was and that they were already ten minutes late. Joining in what I still thought to be a joke I took my own watch from its belt pouch and agreed, as I followed his gaze out over the rolling spinifex. I told him that I made it only eight minutes overdue but it was still cause for concern. If anyone had seen us I'm sure they would have had doubts about the length of time we'd been in the bush, but suddenly Paul's face lit up and he relaxed as he told me that they were at last coming. Sure enough several naked forms appeared from behind a slight mound off to one side and picked their way through the spikey tussocks towards us.

Throughout the time we knew this tribe and including that historic fourth day of August when I made that first contact with them, we never saw any of the women folk closer than several hundred metres away. They and most of the children seemed too shy to come over, preferring to keep a healthy distance from us, but occasionally a small boy would accompany the elders. Having made their approach after laying down their spears 40 metres away, as the two did on my first contact, they would sit in a group near the grader until one of us walked over to interview them. Then almost on cue and without a word, they would stand and amble away collecting their spears as they went. How they knew when to arrive so unerringly at the same time each day we could only guess, probably using the sun, and so each day we began to expect them. On the occasion of Paul's feigned concern we concluded that they must have had some unforeseen prior engagement.

Eventually everything was arranged, with Rex in full possession of the facts, and the next move was up to me to start on the 1400-kilometre trip to Rawlinna. As usual I would travel alone, especially this time as I planned to return with a passenger and half a grader gearbox, so with a few extra tins of meat and some of Paul's freshly baked bread I unceremoniously headed off.

10
Another Gearbox Rebellion

Seven hundred kilometres separated our camp from the Warburton Ranges Aboriginal Mission with nothing at all in between, and the remaining 700 kilometres from there to Rawlinna was just the same. Sandhills, spinifex, and mulga patches made up the sum total of the country all the way, but the first leg of the trip to Warburton was practically devoid of actual sandhill crossings.

Suddenly there was an explosion that brought my Land Rover to an abrupt halt. Even before the dust had cleared, I had begun to plan how I was to handle this fresh situation. I had managed to travel 120 kilometres from the camp at the head of the road skirting the northern end of Lake Disappointment, and to cross over the Canning Stock Route where I had positioned the road alongside Wells 23 and 24. The latter of these also bore the name of Karara Soak, still nestling in the horseshoe-shaped alcove surrounded by the low rocky cliff. That was now 25 kilometres behind my afflicted Rover and although there was nothing there but a well and broken-down cattle trough, it comprised the closest object to me in this almost limitless ocean of sandhills, with nearly 600 kilometres ahead to Warburton.

Such ear-splitting evidence could not, in this case, be interpreted as anything but the final death rattle of the tortured gearbox, which up to now had gallantly dragged its Land Rover across many thousands of kilometres of unexplored wastes in Central and Western Australia.

As if we hadn't had enough dire associations with gearboxes in the previous few days, what with the huge grader lying useless at the head of the road it had just made 120 kilometres back, standing astride a thousand fragments of shattered cog wheels. That self-same raucous clatter had also preceded that recent and instant conversion of a useful implement into an inanimate pile of steel in a most ungainly pose, half-way down that dry creek bank on which it had been working. Any vehicle unlucky enough to be associated with the Gunbarrel Road Construction Party and its isolated activities just had to be pitied and this latest catastrophe helped prove it. If the gearbox remained adamant in refusing to operate at all I looked like being still there for a long time to come, as I could only contact the base station with the transceiver. A lengthy period would have to elapse due to this extreme isolation before any help could be expected from that end. A last resort could be to plod back to the camp, taking several days.

The country to the east of Well 24 was riddled with bottomless boggy stretches of white-capped mud surrounded by sandridges, and this forced me to locate the road close to their banks where the going was heaviest. The grader had smoothed out a passage after much careful reconnaissance to guide it through the maze but the resulting soft surface with its axle-deep wheeltracks must have so increased the strain on the already belaboured vehicle as to spell out an ultimate doom for the gears. It wasn't long after gaining the better surface beyond, which I knew would be with me for almost the rest of the trip, that they had given up the battle altogether. Actually at this stage all that was gone definitely was the third gear position in which I had been travelling, so the next thing to do was to try the others.

No response at all resulted from second gear other than an unearthly repetition of that awful grinding noise. As the vehicle had come to rest partly off the road with great mounds of spinifex in front, I held my breath as I selected reverse. This time the little vehicle answered the call and began to move back along the deep ruts on to the road and once there I already felt much better. I had a dump of petrol drums 350 kilometres away in the direction of Warburton which I was relying on for refueling, but I doubted if I carried enough to reach it in reverse all the way. It was a thought at least.

The powerful but slow crawler first gear was next to be tested and this also was capable of moving the vehicle forward, but once again the petrol supply was too far off to get to it at so few kilometres per litre. Even the camp behind was too great a distance—but the weakest fourth gear was yet to be tried. If successful then it might be possible to get rolling in first and quickly slide to top, bypassing second and third if those wrecked cogs would allow such an operation. I thought of how lucky I was for this not to have happened back in the salt lake belt because if it had there would have been no hope at all. At the first tentative try, the fourth position did make its weak attempt to pull the vehicle forward, enough to inform me that its gear was still intact. Then came the final test, the results of which would determine whether I might reach anywhere, or remain for weeks out in the desert right where I was.

I wasn't really worried either way other than the fact that the road project would be held up and our fourth access link across Australia would have to wait. As before, the vehicle began to creep forward in its first gear, powerfully but only at a walking pace and the time came to change to fourth. It worked and by much misuse of the clutch kept rolling until a reasonable momentum helped and I was once more on my way. Or so I thought.

I formulated a plan that whenever a sandy patch or one of the slight rises appeared I would endeavour to charge it with the greatest speed I could muster, hoping to clear it by sheer impetus. When it became necessary to stop and camp, then it would have to be on a down grade with a hard surface for take-off in front. Everything seemed easy as I travelled along, admittedly at a more rapid pace than I would have liked but at least I was on the move. I couldn't think of anything on this particular stretch of road which might prevent this plan from landing me at Warburton. Even the refueling could be carried out as the sizeable dump of petrol drums was 100 metres off the road clear of fire risk.

It was surprising just how many soft patches did seem to be about, which normally I would have negotiated without even seeing them in a healthy vehicle. With the constant knowledge that not many gears were readily available and there was no allowance for stopping, the small sandy rises appeared as mountains but my scheme was working and I was gaining confidence as each one passed—until late in the afternoon when a long drawn out sandridge which I'd forgotten about came into view.

It was not high by any standard but broad, and the few metres rise proved enough to act as a brake on the extra boost I'd endeavoured to give the Rover. For a while I thought I would make it but right in the centre of the longest stretch with our crew's previous wheel ruts 40 centimetres deep in the soft sand, the vehicle quickly died and became impaled on the high crown between the tracks. The main reason for this was that the smaller vehicle didn't 'track' with the supply truck's furrows and I quickly discovered that neither first or reverse gear would budge it.

The sun was sinking fast, so with what light was left I began shovelling. Mounds of sand built up either side as the high crown was reduced in height, and long channels were carved out behind the wheels. Eventually with these grooves lined with spinifex and the tyres deflated, I was able to back out of the sand on to harder going but as soon as the strain was released allowing more speed, another spine-chilling screech erupted from the mutilated gearbox. This resulted in another dead stop, not from sand but decidedly mechanical as the broken transmission locked the wheels. From now on I knew there was no reverse gear and the only movement I could expect was forward. Those reverse gears are always so taken for granted that when suddenly deprived of them the obstacles seem to be all in front with no hope of backing away, or so I was soon to discover.

Wondering if that first gear which allowed the initial take-offs was working, I tried it out before even recovering my shovel, only to hear a by now familiar and dismal crunch as I slowly let in the clutch. It had now plainly joined the others as scrap metal and was useless also. If the solitary top gear which had already managed to move the vehicle 20 kilometres on its own still worked, then I had another chance. Not that it was strong enough to move the weight of the Rover by itself, but there was yet a further plan I could try. The low-reduction gear was in a separate transfer box and therefore possibly unaffected by the fragments of cog wheels milling about. By combining this with top gear it might take the place of first, and an accurate but hurried change to high ratio using the second lever might allow me to carry on. I only had 550 kilometres left to go. That was, of course, if the lone top gear was still with me.

Selecting top gear with the main gear lever and low ratio with the other, I couldn't help feeling a sense of excitement as I tentatively let in the clutch. It worked. That was all I wanted to know, so I stopped again immediately. Without a great deal more work on that crossing ahead, the chances of passing over it with the vehicle in this condition were very remote indeed and I now no longer had the capability of backing away from trouble. It had to be forward or nothing.

The shovel was still where I'd left it, so I returned to it on foot and set about extending the spinifex-paved wheel tracks and reducing the height of the crown in between. Almost 100 metres would be needed to clear the obstruction and land me on to the harder ground beyond. At this rate it would take months to reach Warburton, but at the same time I really couldn't remember any more bottlenecks ahead. But then I hadn't remembered this one!

By the time the thickly carpeted spinifex road was finished it was well after dark, so after trudging back to the Rover I rolled out my swag on the spot for the night. As much as I wanted to try out my handiwork, I couldn't really dare risk it in the inky blackness of the desert.

With the thought of that crossing ahead and the consequences of the success or failure weighing so heavily on my mind, not much sleep was expected or had during what was left of the night as I lay in the swag rolled out between the wheel boxes in the back of the Rover. As the first faint glow of dawn became apparent on the eastern skyline I was up again and as I tied up the old canvas sheet around the blankets it occurred to me that I could well be undoing it within a few minutes for a wait of several weeks.

The far end of my spinifex-paved road was not yet visible by the time I was ready, so I used the waiting period to walk along and inspect my handiwork of only a few hours before and done by torchlight. The wheeltracks made with a shovel seemed to be roughly parallel and the resulting crown between them was just as I had left it in heaps off to the sides. A little more spinifex and sticks added here and there helped fill in the minutes until the approaching day was unmistakable as the still submerged sun shortened its distance to my visible horizon before actually showing itself. It was now light enough to see everything so I returned to the Rover which was waiting patiently for its turn to prove itself.

Everything had to be loaded on before moving, because once mobile and assuming the crossing could be made, there was to be no stopping at random. The only places must be on hard surfaces with a slight down grade ahead, both of which requirements were not very frequent in this country.

After a warming-up period for the engine to guard against any possibility of a stall during this operation, especially at the time of the unusual gear change involved, all was ready for the attack. With the weakest fourth gear and low-reduction lever engaged, the little vehicle began to move. It was fortunate that it had reached a point well clear of the beginning of the sand before that all important reverse position had given up, because this left just enough room for what momentum I could achieve to be reached.

By the time the front wheels hit the trailing edges of the sandy stretch, they were moving with a reasonable forward impetus and the test was on. I concentrated to keep exactly to the spinifex in the ruts, and before I knew it I was half-way over and as the far end drew closer I could feel the tension build in me as I gripped the wheel as if to lift the weight of the vehicle up bodily. The engine was at screaming pitch within a dozen metres of the oncoming harder ground, although the forward speed was pitifully slow as the drag on the tyres acted like a brake and as the Rover emerged eventually on to the road beyond it was barely moving. Another few metres of that surface would have meant failure and an indefinite camp alone on the desert over 500 kilometres from anywhere.

As the sandy crossing fell behind I soon discovered that I could risk a change into high ratio and be reasonably confident that the momentum would help that solitary top gear to keep the vehicle moving. It was then I realised what an unlikely pose I had assumed with the totally unnecessary help I was endeavouring to give, with elbows out at right angles, shoulders hunched and twisted in the line of the forward motion and lungs fighting for air as breath was withheld. All this while sitting on the edge of the seat with the steering wheel wedged into my brass belt buckle. If I had sat back relaxed as in an arm chair the brave little Rover would have brought me through just the same. As it was it took 100 metres to regain my breathing and normal position so I could execute this gear change I'd been dreaming about an hour before in my blanket roll.

It worked without a sound and the Rover and I were on our way once more. As I went I tried to reconstruct in more detail the events of making the road only weeks before and to remember any similar patches. The main problem which loomed up as my mind's eye brought me to our petrol dump was the fact that I could no longer drive over to it across the sandy spinifex area separating the heavy drums from the road. The road there was our original Gunbarrel Highway where this new road system joined it. Since it was now five years old with that proportion of weathering and traffic, infrequent as they both were in these isolated regions at this stage, it would be harder. Nevertheless there would be no hope of venturing off it with this mutilated gearbox containing only one top gear still working, so the refuelling would have to be done with all four wheels firmly planted on the road surface. That would mean attempting to roll one of the big drums the 100 or so metres over to the vehicle with great hummocks of spinifex trying to block the way with every revolution.

This would also mean a good deal more work but was by no means a problem, as either a shovelled path could be cleared for the operation or the fuel could be carried in a smaller receptacle. As the only other container I possessed was a blackened billy, many trips back and forth would be needed to fill the thirsty petrol tanks involving, according to my calculations, 8 kilometres of walking. Most drivers have easier ways of topping up their vehicles with fuel, but I concluded it was decidedly not impossible. Another way would be to lighten one of the drums by half and roll the easier burden over the humps in one go, but I discounted that method as soon as it occurred to me due to the criminal waste of fuel, made all the more precious by this utter remoteness.

In due course and with no further interruptions or stoppings I cleared the last of the sandridge belt which had persisted since crossing the Canning Stock Route and I knew I had progressed over 100 kilometres from it.

As I drove the invalided single-geared vehicle along out of the sandy valleys on to the open plains I could almost sense ultimate victory, even though 550 kilometres of road was yet to be negotiated. The victory that I had in mind was no longer the arrival at Rawlinna on the Nullarbor Plain and the collection of Rex with the grader parts, but the arrival at the Warburton Ranges Aboriginal Mission, the only place on the way where I could organise help easier than out in the desert.

11
Home but not Hosed

Windy Corner was currently the next goal I had set myself as I broke out of the sandhills on to the open plains, mercilessly beating that life-saving top gear to keep the Rover on the move. Many kilometres went by as I wondered how I was going to negotiate that right-angled bend at speed to enable me to proceed south along the Gary Highway.

There were two possibilities open to me to execute the impending manoeuvre. As the steering wheel again fought to free itself from my belt buckle I knew the familiar feeling of tenseness was returning. As the distance shrank, a decision had to be made and quickly, between charging it at speed and hoping the momentum would carry the vehicle around the corner, or stopping altogether and creep up to it carefully. The second was the sure way, so well short of the corner I stopped and engaged the low reduction lever.

In retrospect it was perhaps not really hard to choose, with the thought of the Rover careering very possibly off the road ahead and landing among the soft hummocks of spinifex, causing a repetition of the long wait on this same spot not so long before. This battle between the vast barren wastes of the waterless Gibson Desert and my all but wrecked gearbox went on unknown by the outside world, I thought as I pulled the low reduction lever back into position. The little vehicle again responded to the combination of the only gears left available to me and I felt thankful as I crawled around the corner and on to the

Gary Highway that we had smoothed out the sharpness of the angle at the junction.

This new 'highway' that I was soon to be driving along had been made earlier than the others, which meant that the wheeltracks were proportionately more established having had many ration and supply trips being made over them during the process of construction. It would make it easier to reselect the high ratio position on this leg of the journey because the vehicle momentum would be maintained longer without so much drag on the wheels, but it still wasn't until I reached a harder part that I attempted the change. I was still on the flat with the southern undulation in front but the weak top gear was able to cause the vehicle to attain a reasonable speed which carried it over easily. I was once more on my way, I concluded, as I settled back into the seat from its edge and relaxed the unusual position I had again assumed.

As the kilometres fell behind, so did the concern for the success of this method of reaching Warburton as it now looked better than ever. The next landmark to reach was the junction where the Gary Highway met the Gunbarrel Highway just south of the Young Range. This was near the northern extremity of the Browne Range, and once on that even more established and harder surface the going would be again proportionately easier. That intersection could be reached if I could nurse the vehicle over the next 180 kilometres and having made the road with the grader only, there were no great sandhill belts to cross. The Young Range wouldn't present a problem as the road threaded through the stony outcrops on an equally stony level surface so the speed could be maintained. One or two twists around individual rock ledges might cause a slowing down but even if I had to stop, the take-off in low ratio would be possible on that section.

Undulations of completely open, treeless horizons came and went and everything seemed to be going well as the first indication of the range appeared on the skyline ahead in the form of Charles Knob. This was one of the stony outcrops which we had decided to use as a future trig hill on the 1958 expedition, forerunner for the location of the

Gunbarrel Highway, and it was already equipped with a permanent survey mark and cairn on its highest point. Although relatively small, it was the highest landmark for hundreds of kilometres around and was linked by line of sight to the neighbouring trig station on the Browne Range at Mount Everard. I had constructed the Gunbarrel Highway to pass the foothills of the latter for easier access by the follow-up survey parties and being the first and only road across Central Australia in those latitudes, I also wanted to make it the shortest, most direct route.

I remembered as I finally reached and passed Charles Knob and saw the equally small Mount Everard 20 kilometres away to the south, how I had arrived at the decision to bypass it in favour of turning due west from Everard with the Gunbarrel Highway. Having progressed as far as the northern extremity of the Browne Range with its construction, five years previously, two possibilities had presented themselves to me. One was to direct the road further north to Charles Knob in order that the survey parties could carry on with their tellurometer traverse by means of a made access, then angle back west-south-west to the next planned rise for the survey, 40 kilometres away. This would provide a road link between these three points and be very acceptable for their work, but would also add 20 kilometres to the overall distance of our new highway. On all our own subsequent supply trips and for that matter any journey future travellers would be surely making, that extra 20 kilometres might mean the difference between negotiating it successfully or not. On numerous occasions when such dilemmas cropped up those thoughts had predominated, resulting in the final location being made along the shortest line. All the otherwise wasted distances when added up on such a huge project amounted to a considerable shortening of the road and it is certain to have brought about the success of the countless trips since made over it.

The overall distance of the Gunbarrel Highway as it stands is 1500 kilometres including the link from the Giles weather station to the main road to Alice Springs, and this could have easily crept to nearer the 2000-kilometre mark, and petrol supplies to get through may not have been able to be carried.

The second course open to me at Mount Everard was to turn the road due west on a calculated bearing to the next tellurometer station rise and leave the following surveyors to make their own way up to Charles Knob. It was easily seen and mostly open spinifex country intervened from Everard but at the same time I remembered clearly how five years ago I had climbed up on to the Everard stony bluff with our home-made map and compass and wrestled with my conscience for two hours. This road would be appearing on all later maps published of Australia and the course of any future progress, as far off as it might be, would be governed or influenced by what was about to happen then and there. A decision had to be made as the bulldozer was returning from his second widening cut from the south.

At the time, our own supply trips had been the first things to consider, to make it possible to even finish the 'highway', and old Bill Lloyd, our current supply driver at that time, would have 40 kilometres return added to every trip. It was a long enough trek as it was, churning along a new, soft, and uncompacted surface. If I had known then that I was later to be making the Gary Highway, there would have been no hesitation in going due west but after climbing down to the Rover at the end of the road to date I had made up my mind to that effect anyway. An almost 50-kilometre stretch of absolutely straight road had landed us exactly on the rise alongside the next planned survey mark decided on by a previous expedition, after starting off on a carefully calculated bearing.

Charles Knob had to wait for its road access for five years but not before being used for the traverse across Australia. The National Mapping boys must have lamented the fact that the road did not visit the Knob but that would have been temporary in comparison with the permanent nature of a made road. Many more travellers, had they known or realised why the Gunbarrel Highway was located where it was, would have applauded the fact just as strongly.

This gave so much food for thought that the distance from the Knob to Everard dwindled rapidly as I urged the Rover along with its sickly gearbox and before I knew it the sign I had made for the turnoff came into view. I had fashioned it the same as the one at Windy Corner, from a large petrol drum with a raised flap, fixed by a broken spring welded from it to the far lip of the drum. Before cutting out the flap with a hammer and cold chisel, I remembered placing the usual aluminium plate with the stamped information flat on the top of the drum in position and with my revolver shooting the holes at each corner, to take the bolts carried for the purpose through both thicknesses. I held the revolver at a distance of a few centimetres while standing on the top of the drum with my face turned the other way, and the bullet had easily penetrated both metals and landed inside the drum. The first shot was quite exciting wondering what might happen to me if the petrol fumes inside might explode and blow it up. I had pictured myself flying through the air to land in a clump of spiky spinifex but the next few shots became routine and a standard method of attaching sign plates to drums at our road junctions. The size .22 bolts I happened to carry just fitted perfectly.

Beyond the white-painted sign were the dozens of drums of petrol in our supply dump, easily seen across the spinifex separating them from the road and I thought how they were near but yet so far. As I reached the junction, this time at speed, and rounded the corner, I was able to stop for the first time since the gear trouble had started with reasonable confidence that I could take off again. That was because I was at last on the hard surface of the Gunbarrel Highway.

The time for refuelling had come, so plodding through the hummocks of spinifex over to the dump, I began pushing at each drum in turn hoping to find a partially filled one to roll over to the almost empty vehicle. One after the other resisted my efforts to tilt their weight without a mighty surge of power and I was fast becoming resigned to shovelling a pathway back to the Rover. With each encounter I was also becoming accustomed to meeting solid resistance and when the same force was applied to the last drum standing apart from the others, I wasn't ready for what happened. The drum was only a quarter filled and as I gave it an almighty shove, it literally soared off over the spinifex, landing me flat on my face among the spikes on the sand.

Picking myself up I realised that although I had some needle extractions to do, my immediate problem was solved. This one could be easily trundled along the very uneven ground to my thirsty Rover.

Using the little hand pump always carried on the Rover, it wasn't long before the tanks were brimful once more and I could continue on with this unique trip. As I anticipated, the take-off was quite easy on the firm down-sloping surface and as I passed by the foothills of the interesting red bluff of Mount Everard 6 kilometres away, the road turned south-easterly towards Mount Beadell. It was 45 kilometres away and every time I approached it from either direction I had the inclination of shyly looking the other way. Although this had become a place name published on the latest maps of Australia, and I realised it was an honour to have my name given to it, it nevertheless caused a sensation bordering on embarrassment every time I drove past it. The red bluff, sheer on one side was admittedly very small by normal 'mountain' standards but the size of such things is very relative. A windrow alongside the road would be a mountain in the eyes of a bicycle lizard but unnoticed by a camel, the same as Mount Beadell appeared as a mountain in these endless horizons of flat spinifex plains but would pass unnoticed among the Swiss Alps.

On a previous occasion when I had been on a solo journey along the Gunbarrel Highway, my vehicle engine had been floundering for days, coughing and spluttering due to I didn't know what, but while it kept me moving I had been reluctant to start dismantling it. The phrase 'if it works, don't fix it' kept repeating itself in my mind until right at the foothills of Mount Beadell where our road skirted it, it chose to give up altogether. After hours of work it began to seem as if I wasn't to find the trouble easily and visions of a cracked cylinder head or worse loomed up, so I contacted the base station at Woomera on the little transceiver after erecting the whip aerial. I told the operator that I had broken down and may be in need of outside help but not until I had exhausted all my ideas of finding the trouble. I would call him later, having now established contact, either when I became mobile again, or required assistance. This could come in the form of a relayed message to my own camp 600 kilometres away at the time, and the boys could drive out on the Gunbarrel Highway to meet me. The operator understood all this and asked me for my present location and I remembered how awkward it had been for me to reply 'Mount Beadell'. He only laughed in his retort about what an appropriate place that was for me above anyone else on earth to spend my last days and perish in the desert.

I had not named the feature myself and was surprised when told that an official naming authority had done so, but being in so isolated a spot it seemed that anyone reaching it could count themselves lucky if they weren't in some form of dire predicament. Even if their vehicle had stood the test, then there was always the thought of diminishing supplies of water, petrol, and rations, or in my present case almost a complete lack of a gearbox. Now here I was again approaching the stone outcrop in a vehicle which normally wouldn't be relied upon to drive to the end of the street in the city.

There was barely time to give the 'mountain' a second glance between concentrating on the road ahead to keep the vehicle momentum going and negotiating the rocky surface as I passed by the great hole we had bulldozed alongside the road which was still there as deep as ever. It was the one we had dug to virtually bury a 3-tonne truck which had need of an entire engine replacement during our construction of the original Gunbarrel Highway. The only way to lift out the great weight with the limited help of a chain hoist was to sink the helpless truck deep enough into the ground to allow us the height available overhead. Another major catastrophe under the shadow of Mount Beadell.

The next 75 kilometres was to my memory completely devoid of any hazard to stop my covering it at the speed required to keep the Rover rolling in that weak top gear. That could then leave me free to worry about Mount Samuel.

It was the stony hill over which I had made the road five years before, because firstly to by-pass it would have meant to clear it with a wide margin owing to the rock strewn slopes tapering out to the desert. This would have necessitated the follow-up trig surveyors reaching the summit through the bush to establish the tellurometer station on the top, thus giving them a lot more work which I was always trying to avoid. When I had done my detailed survey ahead, alone as usual in the bush, to find the exact course that the bulldozer and the resulting road would take, I tried the more direct way by driving over the very top by a winding route through the mulgas. Having arrived within a few metres of the crest where the future survey mark would have to be located, I had continued on down the other side by an equally winding path to fit the road between two smaller rocky bluffs at the bottom. Beyond there had been plain sailing for 75 kilometres to the next visible feature, which was to bear my name.

Top: Last 100 metres to go to bring Gunbarrel Road Construction Party's eight-year operation to a close at Talawana. *Bottom:* Colin Grant's new Talawana homestead near the Robertson Range had same architect as Bill Ellery's Billanooka

ALL NIGHT
CAFÈ
MENU
Beadell.

Being a hard and rock strewn surface, I knew as I drove towards it that the need for charging it at speed would be unnecessary and that the slower low reduction gear should keep the vehicle moving. One short pinch had been more steep than the rest and that was the area which occupied my doubts until camping time. Would the one remaining frail gear pull the weight up even when combined with the low ratio?

The sun was sinking behind me as I neared the twin bluffs between which the road passed, and I could see the bulk of Mount Samuel rearing up beyond, still illuminated by the rays of the sun. If I made it to the top I had already decided to camp on the far side with the Rover positioned on the stones pointing downwards. It was a perfect site for an easy, rolling take-off. Engaging the low ratio lever I soon found that I hadn't anything really to worry about as the vehicle crawled to the trig cairn which had since been piled by the National Mapping parties.

Not stopping until the Rover was aiming decidedly downhill, I climbed out and rolled four large rocks in front of each wheel. I couldn't rely on the gear holding it overnight and didn't have much confidence in the battered hand brake. If it got away it would be the same story as always—stranded in the desert indefinitely, but here at least that much closer to Warburton.

I walked back up to the survey beacon with its magnificent symmetrical rock pile supporting the pole and looked back at the endless horizon to the west from where I had just come. The brilliant orange orb of the sun was by then half submerged below the skyline and there was '*my*' mountain silhouetted against the otherwise flat featureless horizon slightly to the north. To me it was a wonderful scene, remote from anything and everyone, and I knew that in the direction I was gazing there was not a living soul for at least 500 kilometres until the nearest and most isolated cattle station homestead in Western Australia. It was the country which had held a magnetic fascination for me for the past twenty years, clutching me within its depths as a very willing prisoner.

Back at the Rover I decided that I would probably feel

Top: Giles Meteorological Station in 1963, as seen from the top of the radio mast. *Bottom:* Mural painted by author on the mess room wall at Giles a lot less hungry if I ate some of Paul's bread and a tin of meat, after which I could climb into my swag in an atmosphere of complete contentment. The next day would become the big test whether I could reach Warburton mission or not, with only 140 kilometres to go.

Starting off down the hill after removing the rocks in front of the wheels was easy and after passing the turn-off to some rock holes at a brisk pace, I could relax for the 30-kilometre straight run to Mount Charles. The rock holes, full of water at the time I discovered them, were natural and very symmetrical sink holes on a large flat sheet of level rock right at the foot of Mount Samuel. Aborigines had been using them as a fairly reliable source of water, doubtless for generations, and the holes would be replenished after every rain with the run-off from the natural stone catchment. Only after a long dry spell would they be empty and I had made the road to by-pass them by 100 metres to preserve the quiet atmosphere surrounding the area.

Mount Charles ahead would present no problem with my journey as the road wound through several sizeable rock outcrops higher, I'm sad to say, than Mount Beadell but it remained on the same level ground until clear of them. There had been a solid stand of bush between the hills where rain had washed seeds and later nourished growth for thousands of years, but the huge bulldozer had easily carved a path through, leaving a wall of trees and scrub lining this section of the Gunbarrel Highway. It also held one of the tellurometer survey marks now on the higher peak to the north which was the reason for constructing the road so close to it. I could have by-passed the whole feature but that again would have meant a harder task for the follow-up National Mapping surveyors.

Out on the open spinifex and ironstone gravel slopes beyond Mount Charles, the gallant and all but gearless Rover carried me onwards for what I knew to be an uninterrupted section to Jackie Junction. This was a 'T' junction into which I had put a considerable amount of thought for its location 100 kilometres in advance of our road construction from the Rawlinson Range. I had planned to link the Giles Meteorological Station by a road to the Warburton Aboriginal Mission for the first time which would then allow access clear across south-western Australia from Alice Springs to Perth. The 1000-kilometre gap in the existing road systems of Australia would then have been made up by our little party and I planned to tap this road for the last 450-kilometre stretch of the Gunbarrel Highway.

Sandhills and rocky outcrops had made a direct line west from Warburton more difficult and also it would miss our two important tellurometer hills at Mount Charles and Mount Samuel. Sixty-five kilometres north of the mission was the spot I had settled on as the junction, on a particularly open, clean spinifex rise and having fixed the corner by the stars, proceeded then to make the roads conform. This point I later named Jackie Junction, after my youngest daughter who arrived into the world a little too late for other recognition.

It would be easy to round this corner at momentum due to the lack of scrub lining the road and in what seemed like no time the white, lone signpost I had installed appeared in front. It has been often described in journals as the most remote signpost in Australia, which statement at the time was perfectly true. My nightmare journey was almost over when I turned the bend at right angles and headed south towards the mission on the still hard surface of the road we had made five years before.

Whatever happened from then on would be within walking distance of my destination and the distance quickly diminished to the settlement. Crowds of piccaninnies swarmed out to greet me, recognising the Land Rover and shouting at their loudest. I couldn't stop as usual to talk to them until I came to the centre of the small cluster of stone and tin sheds, a thing which at first bewildered them. I would have to explain it all to them in the days to come.

12
A 'Nice' Finish

The original plan of driving all the way to Rawlinna to collect Rex and the new parts for the grader gearbox had now completely changed. Seven hundred kilometres still separated the mission from the railway siding along the Connie Sue Highway which we had made the previous year. Having just struggled that same distance already from my camp with the crippled vehicle, any further movement would be out of the question so after setting up the aerial, I knew I would have to make contact with Maralinga and Rex as soon as possible to inform him of the new situation. Another arrangement needed to be made before he left and this time, as well as a gearbox for a huge road grader, he would need to also include a complete replacement gearbox for a Land Rover.

The offers of where I could stay while I waited came from everyone at the mission, and finally it was agreed that I would sleep in the back of the Rover as usual and have breakfasts with the schoolteacher and his wife, Mark and Roulene de Graaf. The other meals would alternate between the superintendent Ken Siggs, Bob and May Bennett, Barbara and Jessica at the hospital, and Dick and Dorothy Hawthorn. Bob and May were dedicated workers for the Aboriginal people doing just about every job going—like driving the huge ration and supply truck the 1600-kilometre return trip to their nearest rail head at Leonora and helping everyone with everything. Barbara Ridley and Jessica were trained nursing sisters and worked full time in the bungalow-type establishment built as a hospital, treating hundreds of complaints daily as the Aborigines milled about outside in the dust and flies awaiting their turn. Dorothy Hawthorne was a triple-certificated nurse, and she also worked tirelessly in the hospital, while her husband Dick didn't stop from morning till dark also in the cause of the Aborigines.

As a result of the radio negotiations, a truck bringing Rex and the parts would be leaving Maralinga for Warburton after being prepared at Woomera, and although it looked like being weeks in arriving I was not short of plenty to do while waiting. During the months in the desert that year I had been writing the manuscript for a story sharing the experiences of our making of the Gunbarrel Highway with hopeful future readers. Working in the back of the Land Rover at night by lead light from the battery and using ledger books brought for the purpose, I had at this stage finished four chapters of the book, hand written and in pencil. If there was a typewriter at Warburton I could put all this down neatly with two fingers laboriously on paper I'd also brought in a box. Mark de Graaf immediately volunteered his machine, and for the next two weeks my daytime work was assured. The familiar tapping went on all day at a painfully slow pace, interrupted periodically by the happenings at the mission, and by the time the relief truck trundled in I was the proud owner of nearly 20 000 words typed for the first quarter of my book. The paper supply had run out and had to be subsidised with anything I could find, and of course everyone at the mission had proofread the result. Being so unexposed to spelling unusual words for so long, there were many corrections to be made after Mark had his turn, using his classroom manner with ticks and crosses but the general reception gave me confidence to carry on with the project.

This writing all had its beginnings twelve years before when a radio announcer visited Woomera to tape interviews with people at the then exciting new Rocket Range town. I happened to be down from the bush at the time and was included in the interviews. When television reached Australia Bob Caldicott, who was the earlier tape

interviewer, transferred to the new medium and happened to remember that session at Woomera so long before, when collecting guests for a TV talk session. Straight from the bush on a rare trip to Adelaide he contacted me through the Weapons Research Establishment and the live programme took place. The next morning a message came from our Adelaide-based publishing firm to suggest that I drop in for a chat with a view to putting it all down on paper. I gathered up various things like photograph albums, articles for the Woomera paper *Gibber Gabber* which I'd contributed, and bundled them all into a sugar bag as the only receptacle large enough to hold them and dropped in for the invited chat. After a ten-minute lecture from the current editor-in-chief Ian Mudie on how to write a book, I returned to the desert with much more paper than usual for astrofix calculations and began my story one morning at three o'clock. The opening lines came to me as I slept on the canvas among the spinifex one night and fearful that I would forget them, I climbed out of my swag and had half a chapter written by sun-up, when the flies took over to stop me.

Every day upon returning home from the little mission school, Mark would make straight for the typewriter to see what the page number was and how much progress the 'familiar tapping' had made during the day. With this rip-roaring atmosphere surrounding me for so many years I'd decided, long before I began the actual writing, to give the book the title *Too Long in the Bush.*

Periodically, between chapters, I would call up the base station at Woomera on the transmitter to see how arrangements were progressing. I couldn't stay on the air for long as the motionless engine was unable to recharge the battery, but eventually the news came that the truck would be arriving in a matter of days. This made me work harder to round off the typing and finish what I had written, thus completing chapter four. An expert could have done it all in a few hours.

One variation in the venue for the evening meal came in the form of an invitation from two visiting linguists who were to be seen daily sitting in the dust among a circle of Aborigines. For months they had been taking notes for their intensive study of the Pitjantjara way of talking and only in the worst of the dust storms would they retreat into the rock building set aside for their use. This had been labelled in bold letters on a rough plank of bush wood with a name only the Warburton community could think of: 'Language Lodge'. The visiting linguists worked at the mission for a great many months, which showed the dedication of the two ladies who were in their sixties.

I was almost sorry when exactly two weeks to the day, the big relief truck trundled into view across the dusty flat towards our little settlement, barely moving among the solid crush of piccaninnies who had just been released from the school house by Mark. The first few hours was spent in sorting out the load consisting of rations and gearboxes and a start was made almost immediately by Rex to dismantle my Land Rover while I made the rounds of all my hosts with boxes of fresh food. Although this was the last thing they wanted, I had made sure over the transmitter that extra supplies would be included in order that I could replenish their larders which they'd so willingly shared with me during one of the most pleasant two-week's enforced stay in the one place that I'd had in years. Needless to say they were among the first owners of the new book when it was published two years later.

Three days later my Rover was in possession of a brand new gearbox and all back in one piece ready to head back to my camp 700 kilometres away, back over the same roads, being the only ones anyway, which I'd travelled on using a lone top gear.

By the end of the third week since I'd left my camp, we reached old Paul's ration truck, by now very depleted but still quite safe, and the joyful task of restocking it began straight away. The little fridge trailer had been operating as a result of a radio message on our way, in preparation for receiving the fresh meat and items which had been, as usual, frozen solid and packed in an insulated steel box between layers of dry ice. It was still solid as Paul and willing helpers made the transfer.

Rex had already attacked the road grader and with everyone helping, the heavy replacement gearbox parts were lifted on to an old canvas camp sheet under the machine.

While all this advanced mechanical work was going on and having already surveyed the overall length of the road location ahead, I couldn't be of much help, so with the foundations laid for the new book I sat in the Rover and continued writing. It is always easier to add to something than starting from the beginning and by the time the grader was ready for 'road' testing, on the only road for many hundreds of kilometres and which it had just made, I had chapter five completed. One day as I sat in the back of the Rover engrossed in writing I received the shock of my life when my bare big toe was suddenly seized and wrenched from side to side. I dropped the pencil and retracted my foot at such a speed that the three-ply board over my knees and the sheets of paper were hurled in all directions at the same time as a blood-curdling yell erupted into the otherwise deathly quiet desert air. This all had the exact effect that was sought from the incredibly hairy Aboriginal who had crept silently up to my vehicle to play out his little joke. His great hair-covered body filled the opening over the open tail gate and his mouth opened in a burst of laughter, quite rare for the usual run of tribal

Aborigines who usually speak in almost a whisper.

He was the one I had first met on my original lone expedition through this area while planning the course of the road and he had proved even then to be far from the usual run of the rest of his tribe. At that time I had discovered his name to be 'Lolly' and it had taken fifteen years to find that it was actually 'Larlie', a title which set him quite apart from all other members of the tribe. It gave him the equivalent status with them as is associated with a university professor in a white community.

Eventually the time came for Rex to return to Maralinga. By now it was November and the summer heat had descended on us in almost full force when the dust of the rescue truck slowly settled behind it as it disappeared away to the east. We could at last resume our operations in an attempt to complete before Christmas this last road link to the west with 160 kilometres to go. I had planned to put the road between the Poisonbush and Horse Track ranges ahead and there was going to be some carefully planned bends to thread it through the rocky outcrops and sandhills in that area.

We were now back to the days of boiling radiators clogged with dry spinifex husks, which trouble would have been greatly reduced had it not been for the month's delay, allowing the herbage to dry more with the approaching heat of summer. These problems had been part of our lives for so long anyway that it was barely even noticed.

It was good to have a detailed knowledge of the country ahead to the finish, which had been made possible by the position we found ourselves on completing the previous road to the north. In the places I had noted as being worthy of closer scrutiny for a better way around, I spent much time on reconnaissance ahead, and discovered satisfying results to bypass the obstacles found on the original expedition. Even the rough limestone patch which we had no way of skirting succumbed to Doug's big grader blade and we spared the time to grade this stretch three times.

A spate of flat tyres both on my Rover and the huge

grader wheels dogged us for the next three days and these had to be mended in the still persistent wind and dust storms and the heat of the fast-approaching summer. I had five in one day on a forward survey, seemingly mending them from morning till night. Even so the 'geometrical' section of the start of the first expedition neared as the kilometres fell behind and once there I knew we were clear of all the worries of sandhills, limestone, salt lakes, and scrub and the end of the road-making was at last in sight. Everything was looking good and I even had another chapter of my book written.

A completed new aluminium sign plate I had made with all the relevant information punched on to it was waiting to be installed on a diesel drum at the 'T' junction at Talawana. All that was missing was the figure of the final distance back along the new road to Windy Corner and the date which had to be added when the job was done.

With half a dozen kilometres to go I still could not convince old Paul or even Doug and the rest of the party that it would be all over the next day. There was no hope of making them believe me, especially after I failed to suppress a grin as I told them. According to the boys, this road was to never end and must carry on in this desolate waste for ever.

Nevertheless we didn't start the grader engine on the following morning until we had helped Paul and Eric pack up the ration truck with its two trailers. I guided the direction of the grader by the simple method of driving in front slowly along my straight wheeltracks with my Land Rover, which was much more battered than when it had first made them months before. I noticed as I looked around periodically that hot on the heels of the grader and absolutely the first vehicle to use the new road behind it, was old Paul's ration truck, coughing its way through the dust closely followed by the workshop Rover. They told me later that on the offchance I was right, they were surely going to be right there at the finish.

Breaking out of the spinifex on to the open gravel flat near the post-and-wire fence at the old Talawana homestead site I positioned my Rover on the far side of the station road to the Robertson Range. Taking out my camera, I prepared to capture this graphic moment on film for all to see long after it was all far behind us, including the members of the Gunbarrel Road Construction Party who were driving the relatively fast approaching vehicles. I triggered the instrument with 50 metres left to go. In another minute the intervening space had been covered and the link to the far east was through. This was the fourth crossing over Australia's outback my little party had made over the past eight years.

Positioning the grader clear of the junction and regrading that section of the station road, Doug climbed down from the open frame covered in dust clinging to the sweat, and made a laconic remark: 'I was with you at the beginning and I'm still here at the end.'

I guided the ration truck in the direction of the nearby windmill and large stock tank still brimful with limitless good bore water, and at last Paul emerged equally coated with the grader's dust and conceded that this was really the end of the road after all. Looking slowly about him at the tank, windmill, and the ruins of the old Talawana homestead he excelled himself in his praise for the third time this year, only this must have been something special as he slowly said, 'That's *very* nice'.

13
Bush Introductions

The camp that night was dominated by the use of the inexhaustible supply of water from the tank, poured by the bucketful over each other for the first conscience-free bath we'd had since leaving Giles. Out in the desert the few litres of water used for washing was always begrudged by us, however necessary it was after the sweaty days spent in clouds of dust.

Work began next morning with the establishing of the drum-type signpost at the 'T' junction and Doug and I went down to inspect the 'new' homestead of Talawana, one reason being to obtain the speedometer distance to it to add to the sign. People coming from the east on the new road, even if there might only be half a dozen per year for a while, would need to know which way to turn at the junction to proceed with their journey.

The new homestead looked not unlike Bill Ellery's temporary tin hut and was obviously designed by the same architect, but it was deserted on our visit. Colin Grant was out, maybe calling on his neighbour, and we found this to be the case when we made a trip to Billanooka. We left the grader where it was for its return trip to Giles, including a complete regrade of the new road to Windy Corner on the way, for we knew it would be a very long time before it would again receive any maintenance, if ever, and then headed off to see old Bill.

Sure enough Colin was there sitting on the harness-strewn verandah yarning to Bill, as we drove in with the ration truck and Land Rovers. The truck carrying the bulk fuel and tools remained with the grader, as it contained a much less attractive cargo for any possible wandering station Aboriginal. Bill and Colin came out to greet us. I had already described Bill and his house to the party and now at last they could allow themselves to believe me, as also Bill could believe that I really was going to make a road over from the east. He knew that I had survived the desert after seeing a letter I had written to George and Terry while I waited at Windy Corner but as to a road, no chance. I had the feeling that everything we did was so unusual that nobody would accept it until actual results could be seen.

The topic of conversation was taken care of by stories of our latest project until so late into the day that we camped right there on the flat outside the surrounding fence. Our plan was for the rest of the party to return to the grader from here to begin its return to Giles while I went on to Ethel Creek to be interviewed by two officers from the Western Australian Department of Native Affairs about the new tribe I had discovered in the desert. George had spread the word when he had received my letter.

Next morning Bill rustled up a ration sheep which I bought for the use of the party on their way back and we filled the large 1500-litre water tank on the truck, after which we again parted. Our next meeting would be somewhere out in the desert as I didn't then know what the officers from Port Hedland wanted to do but we planned the ultimate return to Giles to be north from Windy Corner to Gary Junction and then via Sandy Blight Junction. I would travel that way to catch up with them when I was finished.

As the party drove off east to Talawana, I drove away to the west to camp the night with Joe Criddle at Walgun and relate first-hand a repeat story of the new road. After a night similar to that at Billanooka but with a new audience, I thought that whoever in the years to come learned of the existence of that new road and made use of it, these three people would be quite surely the first to know, outside our own party.

Next morning I headed north-west to Ethel Creek where

this had all begun and pulled up at the homestead gatepost, still decorated with the aeroplane mudguard. Of course, being an old hand in this part of the country now, I knew all about it.

Terry and George came out, this time also knowing all about me and a complete storytelling session followed for the third time, installed once again in the big leather chair in the 'sittin' room' as Bill would have called it. George was specially interested in the cattle-carrying capabilities of 'out there'. He said you could always tell when a horse was brought up on spinifex tops by the shine on his coat, as I described the never-ending skylines of the spiky clumps. Terry wanted to know all the details of the Aboriginal tribe and on it went until it was time for lunch, which the Aboriginal girls prepared as they had for Iskra.

Early afternoon brought the appearance of Ted Roberts from Port Hedland and Peter Pinker from Marble Bar, who were the officers from the Native Affairs Department sent to learn more about the McKay Range tribe I had happened on in the desert. Aboriginal station hands were brought over to the shade house where the conference was taking place and invited to join in. It was decided that on the following morning I would lead a party in two vehicles back out to the area of the water pool in an endeavour to make further contact with the tribe. The party would consist of Ted, Peter, and several Aborigines, travelling in their departmental Holden utility, while George and I with more Aborigines would travel in the station four-wheel drive Toyota in front. I was quite pleased to leave my tired and battered Land Rover right where it was for the few days rest. Swags were made ready that night and tucker boxes replenished, both items being constantly ready all the time anyway, and pack-camel water canteens filled. With all this activity taking place outside near the station store shed, Terry still wasn't tempted to come, saying she would hold the fort against any stray pilots who might happen to amble in and have food ready for us when we got back. This she would know, as time skeds were arranged for portable Flying Doctor radio contacts which could come from either vehicle. This was going to be a far more elaborate departure from Ethel Creek than I had made on my own months before, and we had now the advantage of a graded road on which to drive—all surveyed, constructed, and waiting.

During the activity of packing Terry came up with a brilliant idea and one which was to cause much hilarity and merriment both before we left and on the trip itself. The station sported a battery operated tape recorder and she decided to have the Aboriginal girls from the kitchen and camp nearby send voiced greetings out to the new tribe in their own language. I tried to tell them in so many words that the desert people were very handsome and would love to hear from them as the tape recorder was produced. This instrument was nothing new to them as they often sent verbal messages to their friends at Mount Newman and Roy Hill or anywhere George happened to be going, but brazenly talking to unknown men hundreds of kilometres away was something else altogether. Gone were the carved wooden message sticks of old toted by nominated Aboriginal 'postmen' or carriers, I thought as I watched the semicircle of giggling Aboriginal girls performing around the microphone. This had to be switched off and on by Terry as their shy laughter drowned out their words. Songs were sung into the tape and coy, hysterically jerky messages we supposed of good will and cheer, were added to the tape 'message stick' as though they were talking to the good-looking men in person. When it was finished and thanks given to them from Terry, they raced away back to their camp to the tune of high-pitched squealing and exhiliration. This was doubled in volume when we called after them to say we would try to bring back replies from the never-never. A former corroboree at the station which had been, with their permission, taped and preserved, was also added to the newly made tape and by dusk all was ready for an early start next morning.

One of the Aboriginal affairs officers was obviously very new to the Department, being much the younger of the two, and I was fast anticipating some 'new-chum' antics from him in the ensuing days. Some of his 'helpful' suggestions were already scathingly dismissed by George who I could see was not going to tolerate too much of this 'city slicker'. It looked like being an interesting trip.

First light next morning saw us already breakfasted and on our way to Walgun where we would stop briefly for a quick mug of tea and leave Joe wishing he was going along. He had some cattle-branding to finish. Bill Ellery thought the steady stream of traffic past his shed would never end as we got to Billanooka, but apart from the mug of tea, he showed no signs of wanting to go 'out there' with us—'too far away from civilisation'.

It was still only mid-morning when we arrived at the stock tank and dry tree still loaded down with millions of finches, and I discovered then from George that it was known in these parts as the 'Dead Horse Mill'. The original horse involved would have been stripped by eagles and dingoes ages before and the desert winds had obliterated any vestige of the bones, but it had served the doubtful honour of giving a name to this spot.

My new drum sign plate was standing alone on the flat at old Talawana in all its glory and our two vehicle convoy turned east after the budding photographers in the party had obtained their 'views'.

It is astounding what a thin thread of a road can do to the rate of progress of a motor vehicle; a graded smooth ribbon thrusting out into the endless rough spinifex, and by late afternoon I could see signs which told me the camp and grader was not very far ahead. Although the road surface was at this early stage as smooth as a table, it was quite uncompacted, a state which couldn't be reached until being driven over after soaking rains many times, and we had already towed the following Holden utility out of several dry bogs. Nevertheless it had done a good job of keeping up to the four-wheel drive by sheer momentum attained by keeping accurately to our newly cut wheel-tracks on the soft dusty surface.

George could also see the evidence of the nearness of my party, none of the members of which he had yet met in person apart from myself, and was clearly eager to see

Top: Leaving Salisbury H.Q. on Empire Day 1951—the first major exploration of the rocket range centre line. *Bottom:* An Avro Ansen makes first landing on a claypan at the '300-mile' point on centre line with supplies for expedition

them in the flesh. During a rough meal near the Emu Range area by the side of the 'road', everyone seemed very agreeable to continue on even after dark for as long as it took to reach the rest of my party and camp with them, having heard so much over the years about the Gunbarrel Road Construction Party.

The rough limestone area with which I had so much trouble on the expedition did not slow progress now, and eventually at an hour before midnight the light from a dying camp fire could be seen ahead. The boys had been certainly making good progress as we were now over 300 kilometres from Ethel Creek, or just over 100 kilometres along the new road. George and I both hit on a joke we would play on the party when we pulled in, about the same time as we saw extra torch lights appear as the boys got up from their swags at the sound of the approaching motors and the glimpses of our headlights.

We planned to stop at the outskirts of the camp and George, who the others hadn't seen at this stage, would climb out to casually ask them 'Does this road go to Alice Springs?', while I crouched down out of sight. Pulling up slowly near the grader I saw Doug armed with a torch amble over with an incredulous look on his face lit up by

Top: Author's survey Land Rover, painted black and white for easy identification from the air, in spinifex at '400-mile' point on rocket range centre line. *Bottom left:* Author with welcome addition to rations. *Bottom right:* Sam Cheshire, who took previous photograph, with same rabbit

our headlights and heard him manage a surprised 'G'day'. George would have won an academy award for acting as he asked his laconic question about the Alice and I could barely suppress a burst of laughter at the expression on Doug's face. He said 'Yeah! but it's a fair way'. George sounded surprised and wondered if he'd have enough petrol for the trip as he had two full jerrycans. Doug politely gave the opinion that he would need more like two 200-litre drums and that if he was wise he'd try to get back to Ethel Creek before he died in the desert. That did it and proved all I could take as I exploded and opened the door of the Toyota. As soon as Doug saw me he saw the joke and laughed so heartily that the Emu Range rang with the vibrations. Introductions were made after the fun died down and all was explained, with the Holden arriving soon afterwards. This drama could never have been enacted anywhere but here in the wilds of the desolate Gibson Desert in central Western Australia, lending the perfect atmosphere to it all.

Paul, not bothering to come over at that time, already had the billy on the remains of the camp fire to offer his guests, whoever they turned out to be, the usual mugs of tea, knowing that in due course when they were good and ready they would be over to meet the rest of the camp. It must have looked a little odd to an impartial observer, all this activity taking place in the middle of these dreary wastes and to add to the scene, all around midnight.

The Aborigines from both vehicles produced their tin mugs and while we prepared to camp for the night, they showed no signs of settling down any further from us than a few centimetres. The whites of their eyes could be seen in the firelight as they darted frightened glances out into the blackness beyond. They were visibly very disturbed at the thought that 'bush blackpell' were about, as they remembered the reason for their trip and refused to budge from the fire circle. The mysterious unknown to them was a factor governing their whole way of life with beliefs in Dreamtime spirits and associated rituals, and we could understand their fear on this occasion. In broad daylight and if we did encounter the tribal Aborigines face to face, we knew it would be another story, however strange for both sides the meeting would inevitably be. Even so there was not much sleep to be had by the station Aborigines that night as we heard them huddling even closer to each other and us throughout what was left of the night.

Paul was up even before George next morning with the fire going and chops from Bill's ration sheep already sizzling in our big frying pan for the enlarged camp. Anxious to get going and as far as the new officer was concerned, to be back out of this area as soon as possible, we left Doug and the boys to the regrading and drove ahead of them to the east. The road ahead of course had only been cut once at this stage but was still far better than the original untouched surface.

The area of the McKay Range and the country of the newly discovered tribe wasn't really so far onward and we stopped at the site of our old month-long camp where the broken-up gearbox was restored. At this place constant contact had been made with the Aborigines over a longer period than where I first found them on the expedition. That first sighting was a little further south, near to the water pool among the ranges, so we carried on in that direction after informing the Ethel Creek Aborigines that we were now in the country of the unknown tribe and to watch out for signs of them. We didn't have to wait long before excited fists pounded on the roof of the cabin to indicate that we should stop. Following the direction of their wildly gesticulating and pointing fingers, George and I saw the object of their attention in the form of a cloud of birds, mainly galahs, hovering close to the ground near some rocky outcrops a few kilometres off to the north. 'Prob-ly rock hole!' they yelled as the Holden pulled up behind us and although this was in the opposite direction to my large pool to the south we headed off towards the open-air aviary.

The clearance on the Holden wouldn't allow it to negotiate the high spinifex hummocks and we left it on the road, making it necessary for all of us to climb aboard the Toyota on its truck-like tray among the petrol and swags. The young officer was wearing 'scuffs', as George put it, for he had the first of the run-ins with him on the spot because of them. He became quite heated for the first time since I'd known him, as he told him he couldn't walk over the desert in the event of a breakdown and he sure wasn't going to carry him. The new chum maintained he could but still was flatly refused a place on the Toyota and at the height of the flare-up was forced to remain with the Holden. I could see the beginnings of just such a confrontation ever since they met at Ethel Creek and the scuffs supplied the excuse.

The birds were still very much in evidence when we neared the rocky jump-up and we wound around the foothills to the spot which seemed to be mainly attracting them. Leaving the vehicles clear of the large fallen rocks we walked into a deep crevice and sure enough a sizeable basin-like sheet of smooth stone appeared which was thickly covered with white droppings from years of bird visitations. Reaching the lip of the basin after walking over the sloping rock surface we saw a large pool of water covering the bottom of the bowl. Black and slimy with some bleached bones lying around the edge, it was nevertheless water, a priceless commodity in these otherwise barren wastes. This looked like being of perhaps a more permanent nature than the much larger one I had discovered on that eventful morning just before I had met up with the tribe, due to the nature of the impervious receptacle compared to the dirt bed of the watercourse. Any shower of rain which passed by this rocky place would all be channelled into this depression with the quick run-off and as it was shielded from the sun for most of the day by the surrounding hills, evaporation would be reduced to a minimum. It was a perfect place for the tribal Aborigines to resort to in times of drought which was *all* the time out there, and a natural sanctuary for birds and animals as well.

Leaving it once again to the pink mist of squawking galahs, we retraced our tracks over the whitewashed rocks to the Toyota. The station Aborigines were way ahead of us and greeted us with renewed excitement and with news of their latest discovery. Leading us over to a small stand of mulgas they pointed to the uppermost branches and yelled 'bungarras'. There, wedged up in the forks out of reach of dingoes, were several bundles of bound bark and grass tubes with goanna and lizards tails protruding from the ends. These had been roughly cooked or singed in a fire and stowed away for future use, which the Aborigines assured us would be that same afternoon judging from the freshness of the bare-foot tracks in the dirt. They guessed that with the noise of our approaching vehicle, the owners of the bungarras must have gone bush, disturbed in the preparation of their meal.

The first inclination was to follow the tracks with the Toyota but this was quickly suppressed by our Aborigines who knew very well that we would have no hope of catching up with the mysterious nomads, a thought I had when I had first found the tribe. Sit down and wait was the logical thing to do, as I had previously, and we were assured they would turn up in due course with their own curiosity getting the better of them. They would well remember that day three months before when I had made the first contact with them which had resulted only in friendship, so with that we put on a billy for lunch, a little removed from the area of the bungarras.

I was thinking that if unseen pairs of eyes were watching us, they might recognise me at least and that might speed up our inevitable meeting, but this was not to be the case as we found after only an hour's wait.

Sure enough just after our dinner camp, our Aborigines still sitting almost on our laps, whispered 'black-pell bin comin' now', long before we were aware of their approach. The Ethel Creek boys sat in the dry creek bed pointedly looking in the opposite direction in a most awkward pose as we stood up to greet the two fine looking naked youths walking towards us from behind the nearest of the rocky hills. They showed no outward hesitation or fear as they strode over and I could see straight away the reason for the hour's wait. They were not among the members of the tribe present at my earlier meeting, although in this country obviously connected with them; they probably had been away hunting in an area removed from the spinifex fires which had led me to the others. The story of our meeting would have been told to them when they rejoined the tribe of course but these hadn't actually seen me for themselves.

They were very well built in comparison with usual desert Aboriginals and we guessed them to be in their late teens. One had a pattern of large weals covering his chest and upper arms which was the result of deeply cutting long slashes into the skin with sharp slivers of broken stone and filling the open wounds with handfuls of white ash from their fires. It heals into high ridges as part of a visual proof of some special ritual, as was explained later. He also had a hole pierced through the septum of his nose and as we greeted them, they showed remarkably white strong even teeth in a broad smile.

Our Aborigines made no move to even turn around and remained in the creek bed with their eyes glued to everything but the new arrivals and seemed almost embarrassed at their presence. The two bush teenagers in turned ignored their 'cousins' to the extent of hiding behind us as if they hadn't even noticed their presence.

We all knew that in their own good time, a very formal meeting would surely soon be taking place.

14
The Official Interview

The two bush boys at last deigned to saunter over and sit on the ground in the creek bed within fly-swapping range of our Aborigines as if they had only just happened to notice their presence. They oriented their line of sight as they casually sat down to study a rock in the opposite direction and there the two groups filled in a melodramatic period of time, back to back, each waiting for the other to make the first move. Finally one of the station Aborigines managed a tentative whisper.

The immediate response indicated that the ice had been finally broken and in no time excited but still whispered exchanges were drifting back and forth until they decided that it was time for them to actually turn around and look at each other. Not in the eyes, of course, being far too early in this encounter, but still it was at least a start.

I was dying to ask questions through our expert interpreters as to whether these were from the original tribe, if they knew of our earlier meeting, and what contact if any they already had with 'white-pel'. The station boys quietened me down with a look as much to say 'all in good time' and we had to just watch the proceedings in patience not understanding a word of the rapid bursts of whispering. Eventually they decided the time was right and I was allowed to put forward my queries, to which the answers were much as I had imagined they would be. They were members of the group I had encountered on the expedition and they did know all about my passing visit and the subsequent long camp in their country where we repaired the grader gearbox. Also with regard to previous 'white-pel' sightings, I was told that they had never seen any before and that 'you bin first time'.

Asking the whereabouts of the rest of their people, we got the impression that if they were allowed to brave the motor vehicle by climbing on it, they would guide us to them 'long way'. Following the direction of their out-thrust bottom lip as is their way of pointing, I quickly concluded that the others were probably in the area of my large waterhole on the southern side of the road.

To add a little relaxation to this scene I pointed to the hole in the chest-decorated boy's nose and playfully broke off a stick and tried to put it through my own. Screams of laughter followed this and he joined in the fun by diving on a green twig which he snapped off to a suitable length and inserted it properly through his nasal aperture. This definitely had to be photographed and I again slowly took out my camera, showed it to them, and proceeded to obtain a record of this moment. Looking through the view-finder, I could see the stick was not exactly bisected by the loop of skin through which it was pushed, so walking over to him I gently tapped it through a little further to even it up. This action was received with glee from the other boy who by then was rolling on the sand in hysterics. We were certainly off to a good start—and our Aborigines helped them on to the bonnet while everyone else took their usual places.

The bungarras in the tree were temporarily forgotten as we slowly retraced our wheeltracks to the road and the waiting be-thonged young officer in the Holden. Once there half of the passengers reverted to their own vehicle and with our two newly found friends pointing the way we drove off in the direction of their extended lower lips.

Again as I thought, we branched south off the road towards the gap in the McKay Range through which I had escaped from the basin just before I had made my first contact with these most remote people. This time the distance to the range was much less than it was to the galahs and the Holden attempted to follow in our wheeltracks with some success as we skirted the higher of the clumps of spinifex. In a short time we reached the camp of a small family on the banks of the watercourse leading from the gap and my large waterhole which was now reduced to a dusty basin.

The camp consisted of two very old women, three small children, and an old man to whom we immediately gave the name Charlie and who was already known to me, being one of the original members of the group I had seen first. As I deduced then, he was the comedian of the tribe who would interrupt his long excited harangue with peals of almost toothless laughter as he pounded his thighs before falling to the ground helpless with uncontrollable laughter. Whatever he had been saying must have been funny only to him as the others hadn't shared in his exhilaration at all, and it had only been after I'd drawn a sketch of one of their skin and bone dogs and given it to them that they joined in.

If I had been in my Land Rover he would have known me immediately as it had been the first and only vehicle he had seen in his life, but as soon as he recognised me as I climbed out of the Toyota he rushed over and threw his arms around me, laughing loudly as he did. The old women sat by their microscopic fire cackling in an equally toothless expression of disbelief at this sudden intrusion, and appeared as would their European sisters in the city when totally unprepared for guests. The sound of our engines had informed them that we were about, even before the drive off to the north and probably knew it wouldn't be long before we came over to their camp, not that we knew where it was until finding the nosepeg boys.

The three piccaninnies were shyly sitting in the creek bed by a moist-looking hole they had dug, which had at its lowest part a puddle of muddy water only a few centimetres deep. This was obviously the camp's water supply left over from the former rains which had filled the channel in the basin and had since seeped in below the surface of the sand and dirt. George offered them a biscuit each from a packet he had opened and generally passed them around, and feeling quite hungry as usual out here in the bush I took one also. Charlie took a handful and just as I was about to take a bite my attention was temporarily centered on the old women examining their biscuits, leaving my hand poised half-way to my mouth. At the instant I continued to raise my biscuit I felt a tug and looked around just in time to see it disappearing into Charlie's mouth as my empty fingers automatically carried on to my face. He had whipped it clean out of my hand and swallowed it in one lightning stroke and George didn't stop laughing for an hour describing ever after the incredulous and surprised look which I apparently had assumed as I stared wide-eyed and open-mouthed at my empty fingers.

At the sight of the meagre supply of water the young officer from the city produced a canteen and gave them a tin full of the clear liquid as he placed the screw cap on the mudguard. Old Charlie gave this operation his undivided attention and after the old women were safely in possession of the water, he grabbed the cap from the Toyota and set about trying to replace it on the threaded spout. He had seen it being turned off and concentrated on repeating the performance resulting in hopeless failure and was duly shown how to screw it on. This had to be tried again so Charlie proceeded with the same action as he had just seen but still to no avail. 'No, no!' said the new chum city officer, 'to take if off again you must turn it *anti*-clockwise.' It was a purely automatic statement but it was not only George this time but the rest of us whose eyes flooded with tears of laughter at the way old Charlie stared at him not understanding a word, so completely ignorant of the intricacies of screw threads. Even though he couldn't see the joke he also joined in and the scene was utter bedlam while we all roared and the unfortunate officer was never to hear the end of his blunder for the rest of the trip. The old wild Aboriginal had never even heard of a clock.

Some discarded station clothes had been put into a box by Terry to give to the tribe if we again caught up to them, a reunion which was by no means definite when we left Ethel Creek and these were now taken from the open tray of the Toyota. George handed Charlie an old pair of riding trousers which he examined, then came over to me pulling at my shirt. A new outburst of hilarity erupted even including the nosepeg boys as Charlie tried to pull them down over his head and push his arms through the trouser legs. This didn't seem to work at all and he took them off again to re-think the next try by comparing the shape with George's clothes this time, as my shorts didn't look anything like the article he had. We could all see that the light had dawned suddenly as he held them up by the waist allowing the legs to hang down over his own, and he proceeded to put them this time on the right end. This operation left us helpless once again as he lay on the sand between the spinifex with his legs pointing skywards and proceeded to pull them *down* to his waist endeavouring to thread his feet through the flopped over twin tubes. Even the old women were left rolling in the dust, cackling louder than ever and the piccaninnies had by now climbed up the bank out of the creek and were part of the audience at this outback, open-air vaudeville show.

Then came Terry's *coup de grâce* which had temporarily been put into the background by the events so far: the tape recordings from the Ethel Creek house girls and their corroboree. During a lull in proceedings and while we all tried desperately to regain our breath, George took the instrument out of its sponge rubber-lined box and set it up on top of the front tyre out of sight under the mudguard and pressed the 'play' button. Suddenly the sounds of giggling girls interspersed with silvery words in their own language or at least close enough for them to understand, wafted from our vehicle. Charlie froze in his tracks and listened with his head cocked while his hands on the ends of his spidery arms slowly flexed into fists. Not only did he quieten but so also did the whole of the Aboriginal population present with the atmosphere such that you could, given a suitable floor, hear a pin drop.

With his feet rooted to the ground, Charlie slowly twisted in the direction from which the voices came and the semi-whites of his eyes could be seen under his beetling forehead as the lids dilated to their full extent. The old women gasped, dropped some sticks they had been about to push into their fire, while the children and the nosepeg pair all stood where they were and stared at the mudguard with their sagging jaws leaving black holes in their faces.

It was Charlie who was the first to rally out of his rigid pose and as we silently watched, he crept cautiously to the front of the Toyota doubled over with his arms straight out behind him. Checking that there were no other people secreted away in the vehicle he circled, searching under and over it, gradually converging on the origin of the voices. Not one of the assembled onlookers moved a muscle watching this unprecedented of scenes. On his knees Charlie crawled half under the engine as the girls voices bubbled on with their messages which he seemed to assume were directed at him personally. Straightening up to his full but diminutive height at last, he began answering them back, taking advantage of the occasional pauses and warming to his task added the appropriate actions to his words. It wasn't long before he was shouting at it and dancing about in the sand, gesticulating with fists flying and generally putting on an act worthy of a high-ranking comedian. Only this was not an act. He was quite serious while at the same time enjoying it all immensely, and slowly the other Aborigines drew closer, uttering amazed gasps and whispering probable opinions to each other as to what was going on.

Then came the taped corroboree segment and this reaction made us lament the lack of a movie camera among our gear. The desert Aborigines actually joined in with dancing and miming the words and their prancing feet soon had a patch worn away alongside the front wheel from which dust swirled and was kicked about in all directions. This was top entertainment worthy of top billing on any stage show anywhere in the world, made doubly all the more perfect by the spontaneity of it all out here in the desert many hundreds of kilometres from city theatres as they ad-libbed their way through the performance.

Distracting Charlie's attention to another handful of biscuits on cue when the tape came to the end, George depressed the 'record' button. We carried on our one-sided conversation with him while the station Aborigines, knowing what was going on, kept relaying messages backward and forward between other members of the group. We asked Charlie if he thought he should be given a vote to ban the bomb and the ten-minute reply was decoded to tell us there were more lizards to be found further along the creek bed. The more seasoned Aboriginal affairs officer, once we had set the scene for the interview, added his comment that the hole in the nose of the other Aboriginal must have been a five-eighth's clearance to accommodate a nine-sixteenth nose peg. That reply brought home the fact that the bulk of the tribe were off over the ranges hunting. All this while the tape recorder was silently running under the mudguard.

At a suitable point in the proceedings, George manipulated the buttons and set the machine to repeat all that had just taken place. Charlie's voice together with the nosepeg boy's wafted out from the top of the wheel and it was on again. Remembering of course what they had just been saying, although our voices meant nothing but a background noise, the desert people reacted to this new utter magic far exceeding our expectations and once more we wished this could all be shared by more than just our little party. I couldn't help thinking there and then 'Good on you, Terry'.

The sun was still relatively high above the western horizon and the two officers thought there might be enough of the day left to make a good impression on the trip back to Ethel Creek. As professionally pleased as they were at actually having met some of 'my' tribe, neither wanted to prolong this excursion any longer than necessary in this November heat, and resolved to return in more congenial weather to resume their study. This being the case we prepared to make our departure from our desert friends after having our Aborigines relay to them the future intentions of the Department of Native Affairs in that section of country in Western Australia controlled by them.

George wanted to drive up to the crest of the first of the

nearby ranges to 'see what was on the other side of the mountain' before retracing the tracks back to the road, so with our complement of passengers we began the ascent. In the meantime the Holden slowly and carefully picked its way back to the graded track and waited for us there.

The slope was strewn with loose stones and small rocks, but the four-wheel drive fought back and with two station Aborigines sitting on the bonnet we quickly rose up above the level of the plain behind. Even the Aborigines accustomed as they were to this sort of vehicle, showed some signs of doubt that it would make it to the top, but on and up it went at an alarming angle. I decided also that I wouldn't have attempted this manoeuvre had I been on my own as I usually was, but eventually we flattened out at the top to see a vast sea of the rugged rocky ridges of the McKay Ranges. George yelled out from the cabin that he was going to drive on down the other side but the Aborigines on the bonnet who could see more ahead in the immediate foreground threw up their hands in a terrified action and shouted 'Nothing more!! too 'teep'.

We opened the doors and walked around to the front to see that the way ahead was of a certainty 'too steep', being in reality a vertical cliff. With outwardly suppressed bush humour, George shrugged that off and told the boys that we could easily go down there, 'nothing to it', he returned to the cabin, and revved the engine. It was a case of 'now you see them, now you don't' as in a flash the two Aborigines vanished from their place on the bonnet to stand well clear off to either side to watch the fun.

Of course instead of lurching forward to plummet down over the cliff ahead, he reversed away from it and turned the Toyota around. I helped to add to the illusion by also climbing back into the cabin and positively slamming the door. When the boys saw what was happening they looked almost disappointed to be robbed of the spectacle of the vehicle flying end over end through the air to disintegrate on the rocks below. They wouldn't have brought into their calculations then just how they, as they shot off the bonnet, would be able to return very easily to the station if that had happened, looking ahead only as far as the imminent excitement.

Only when the vehicle was aimed well away from the cliff did they consent to resume their place in the back tray and in due course we were back on the flat on our way over to the road, with George still chuckling at the ridge behind which was 'too 'teep'.

In the time we had been away to the south, Doug and the boys in my camp had already graded past our turn-off and I knew that I wouldn't be seeing them again for some little time. Actually it was to be ten days before I caught up to the mobile camp but there was no hurry anyway.

Off into the west we drove at an even improved rate as we had the advantage of our outgoing wheeltracks on the graded surface to use after we had cleared the newly graded surface back to the site of their camp the night before. The limestone patch passed almost without notice as did the Emu and Wells ranges and soon we were again driving between the Poisonbush and Horse Track ranges.

It came as a relief when the glaring sun dipped down below the western skyline because driving straight west it appeared more as an eye-torturing arc-welding light as it hovered just above. By our speedometer it was becoming more and more obvious that we might with some effort reach Talawana before camping, so with all agreed, especially the following officers, we pushed on in the cool of the evening. Before we realised it, the headlights picked out the aluminium sign plate on the drum at the junction and we carried on without even stopping the few hundred metres to pull up at Dead Horse Mill. It was time for a tea camp being around midnight by then, and it was increasingly evident that we might even go the rest of the way afterwards to sleep right back at Ethel Creek.

We made a fire while George, even at this late hour, mixed up some flour and water to cook some Johnny cakes in the coals. I would have been inclined to open a tin and carry on if I had been on my own but then I surely wasn't in the habit of driving about this country once the sun had gone. Sometimes it seemed the best thing to do but more often than not I had to stand up to a theodolite and spend the night reading angles on to stars, between the mending of the never-ending succession of flat tyres.

Quantities of peach jam were smeared over the resulting and really excellent Johnny cakes, or Survey cakes as we would have called them, and a big black billy of tea was shared to finish the welcomed meal off. After this we reboarded our respective vehicles by common consent and headed off for Billanooka. Bill was already out on our arrival and after more tea and animated exchanges about our desert trip, we carried on in the blackness to Walgun where Joe refused to allow us to pass without yet more tea and a run down on our experiences.

It seemed to me that this was all a repeat performance of my return from the desert with the road and after promising Joe a more detailed encore later we pulled out for Ethel Creek.

At almost three o'clock in the morning the lights of the homestead winked through the mulga without the aid of our headlights. Terry had already been contacted over the transceiver and was expecting us which was very nice as long as she didn't have more tea at the ready; a feature of the bush being so ingrained that we knew she would have anyway.

Everyone, especially those on the following vehicle, was by then coated in a thick crust of dust and sweat and as the Aborigines melted into the night to head for their camp we plodded into the 'sittin' room'. As if people at times even in the bush never slept which was certainly not the case, we flopped down to give Terry an outline of the trip and its success at having met up with the tribe or at least some of its members. Nobody could do justice to the tales about Charlie at this hour and Terry ordered us all to our swags knowing she would get the whole story all in good time.

15
A Life-Saving Decision

By station standards late next morning, we were all up again for once *after* the sun and when the cook girls brought over breakfast we told them all to come over to the shade house to listen to the tape recordings brought back from the desert. The whole episode was relived as they assembled after the meal to hear Charlie go through his routine to the shrieks of delight from the girls and the rest of their families when his words scratched their way through the little speaker. Over and over it was played to their repeated requests for encores and each time the shade house vibrated to their shrill squeals as new words missed previously because of the noise, came over to them.

Terry waited patiently, joining in the fun until it had all subsided and she could hear details of the whole story of the trip. Little did she know what my lone visit now months before would lead to and I suppose on thinking about it, neither did I.

Vowing to return to conduct a further study and take a census for the records, the two officers from the Department of Native Affairs, Ted and Peter, drove off bound for Marble Bar and Port Hedland after mid-morning mugs of tea. As they disappeared in clouds of their own dust George muttered something to the effect that he hoped their scuffs went with them.

The afternoon was occupied with the education of a selected station Aboriginal boy in the art of cutting stallions, of which there were several waiting to convert into geldings, and I went over with George to the horse yards. Even after such a recent and long trip, work on the station must go on. Roping the wild-eyed bush horses came first and they were tied in a most ungainly pose to the heavy post and rail enclosure and from his belt pouch came George's razor-sharp knife. In the next few minutes I don't know who received the more educating, the Aborigines or I, but having operated on one George handed his knife to the Aboriginal boy saying 'You can do the rest'. With that he climbed through the fence and into his Toyota as I followed, quite amazed at the brevity of the lesson. Driving back to the station George told me that's the best way to teach, as he put it with 'shock tactics'.

As if there were never a dull moment at Ethel Creek, no sooner had we pulled up near the store shed than a cloud of dust appeared behind another vehicle to herald the arrival of William Holden from Balfour Downs. His radio transceiver had given him an hour-by-hour description of our activities of the last few days and he knew we had returned from the desert by listening in to our skeds with Terry. Not to be left out of all this exciting news he had come on over and of course stayed to tea and camped the rest of the night, leaving George and I to sleep in the shade house.

During the evening as we talked I happened to notice a typewriter tucked away on a table in the corner of the big room and this gave me an idea. I had written another chapter of *Too Long in the Bush* since the grader gearbox drama. The first four chapters were safely in my box which I had laboriously typed at Warburton while waiting for Rex after that mammoth top gear trip and I resolved to add a typed chapter five to the total before leaving. Terry was an expert typist already, but during the following day she preferred to read what I had already written while I pressed on with my two fingers. That made her only the second person to offer an opinion of how it was going, as Mark de Graaf had already checked some of my spelling at Warburton, leaving her the first mortal ever to read chapter five after I waded through the typing.

This operation couldn't begin until I'd accompanied

George out to a remote bore on the station to help start an engine pump because of the lack of wind for the mill. The cattle trough was not going to be filled for a long time from the stock tank alongside, being almost empty in the calm hot days while we'd been away.

The typewriter slowly clacked away for the rest of the day in the cool darkness of the homestead while Terry assumed the role of editor reclining on the huge leather divan. The outside temperature was 44°C and it seemed to me not only an opportunity to add some typed manuscript to my book but also to escape from the mid-November heat, however temporarily. Our whole lives revolved about work necessarily done in the open whatever the conditions were and while we didn't even think about it, a brief spell was easy to take.

Terry just had time to finish reading and giggling over my mis-spelt words in the completed typed pages of chapter five when another vehicle engine could be heard coming from the opposite direction of the other visitors. Everyone seemed to arrive at meal times (it was now midday on the following day) and we went out to greet the Roy Hill folk who also had been in on all this activity by means of their radio. A first-hand account was sought by them and the ritual went on all that afternoon in this most well-used room in the homestead, while their vehicle simmered out by the gate in the blazing heat.

The time had come next morning for me to finally leave to rejoin my camp out in the Gibson Desert wherever they may be by now, although I was very gratified to sense that George and Terry were reluctant to say goodbye. We had built a real bush friendship including the sharing of a long hard trip out to the desert which is always a great leveller, but we all knew the move had to be made.

According to my calculations my party would be in the vicinity of Windy Corner in about a fortnight from when we had last seen them near their Emu Range camp. There was nothing I could do until the regrade was finished and the team had started the long return to Giles with the grader blade 'up' at last, so I had been contemplating returning to them via the Gunbarrel Highway. This would save again travelling east over our new road so soon after the last long trip and would serve as a change of desert scenery. I could also see how our older road, finished now just five years previously, was faring under the weathering and traffic, since I had heard reports of a number of people venturing out over it as it became more well known. I didn't know as I made that decision at Ethel Creek that this would mean the saving of a man's life.

This meant I would retrace my tracks from the turn-off of the sacked station hands when I first entered this area and drive south to Meekatharra on the Great Northern Highway. From there it would be east to Wiluna and on to the start of the Gunbarrel at Carnegie Cattle Station homestead, about 1000 kilometres from Ethel Creek in all. It would serve several purposes including the saving of the camp's rations and meagre water supply in my absence while the regrading was proceeding. Once that was done and they'd reached Windy Corner, it wouldn't matter.

As we walked from the homestead to my Land Rover, I suddenly realised I hadn't moved it since pulling into the station just after we'd finished the road. After refuelling, no more preparations were needed. It was self-contained and at the ready all the time and after warm handshakes with George and Terry I experienced a certain unwillingness to climb into the cabin. There didn't seem to be any prospect in the immediate future of seeing them again and I wasn't to know as I started the engine that fifteen years would elapse before we would once more meet. Also that after our reunion only a month would pass before receiving word that George's brother, ex-inspector Bert Anderson who was at our meeting in Perth, had died.

Right then I knew I had a very long way to go and after promising them that one of the first copies of *Too Long in the Bush* would be in the post to them when and if it was ever published, I drove slowly off towards Meekatharra. Apart from the waving George and Terry seen in the newly adjusted rear vision mirror, I picked out the brightly painted aeroplane mudguard still adorning the gatepost, the first thing which I remembered noticing on that freezing July morning.

I also knew now that there never had been a ruthless ogre at Ethel Creek as I made the turn at the tree under which those station hands had been sitting. I remembered how they had taken my offer of some valuable rations I could have well used while waiting for days at the end of my expedition on the Gary Highway in the dust storm, but that was in the past.

My plan had been to make an easy trip down and camp in the Rover wherever I happened to be by dusk and get back to the early nights again after all the upheavals to our normal routine. That was until I happened on a car obviously stranded by the side of the road with its bonnet up in the shimmering heat. It was pointing in the same direction as I was going and I stopped to see if I could help. Nothing else could be seen to the horizon in any direction and as I walked over I saw it was occupied by an elderly couple, sitting helplessly inside stewing in the oven-like cabin.

They told me how they had been driving along and stopped for a drink from their water bag after which the engine refused to restart. In fact nothing had happened at all when they tried and there they sat waiting for someone who might be also stupid enough to be using the highway in this heat. Thanking them for that and saying I was just such a person, I knew what was wrong in a flash as anybody who had been associated with as many dirty battery terminals as I have, and proceeded to the engine with my geological hammer in hand. Everything was too hot to handle so after a couple of light taps on the connections I told them in my most professional way to 'give her a go now'. Of course it burst into life immediately as I knew it must after sighting the messy acid powder build-up on the battery, and I shut the red-hot bonnet. They were so grateful they asked me to follow them to their place further down the road for lunch; a suggestion which I quickly accepted as the time taken to make the invitation was filled with the roar of their engine in case it stopped again.

We had already introduced ourselves and at the sound of my name his ears pricked up and he said, 'Not from the

Gunbarrel Road Construction Party?' I assured him I was but in turn their name of Tom and Mrs Parkinson didn't bring about the reaction from me as he expected in this part of the country, because I didn't yet know that he was the owner of a working copper mine.

Off we went with me trailing behind in his dust until we came to an impressive turn-off to the west near a place called Kumarina. Driving in along a road bordered with neatly white-painted stones, I could soon see the shape of a huge gantry with conveyor belts and large engines alongside an array of outbuildings and a main house, and wondered why we were going there first but this was explained as he came over to me. This *was* his place and he owned everything in sight and told me he would show me over it all after the meal.

While his wife stayed well indoors out of the heat, Tom took me over and showed me ore samples and bags of his fertiliser product ready for sale, which was a main result of his copper-mining operations and even though he did appear elderly, he certainly didn't act like it as he clambered over the rigging with me in pursuit. I asked him if he had anyone to help with all this heavy work and apparently he had one man but didn't know where he was right then since he'd been away for a day or two. On the ground once more we walked across the dusty expanse towards one of the outbuildings and on rounding the corner both of us saw the man at the same instant.

Lying on his back in the dirt in the blazing sun with his mouth gaping was the helper he had spoken of sprawled with arms and legs in all directions and apparently lifeless as clouds of flies attacked his open mouth. I said 'Great Scott' and Tom said 'No, that's Alby Coonan'. We rushed over and felt for a pulse which surprisingly was faintly present, after which we half carried and half dragged him into the shade of the nearest shed. When we first reached him the thing which surprised me was his teeth, laid bare by his retracted lips. They were jet black. At first I thought it had been due to the flies but after brushing them off they still resembled rough ebony stumps guarding the wide-open cavity, which we tried to close by pressing upwards on the lower jaw. I raced to my Rover for a tin of water while Tom loosened a grimy shirt worn under a ragged coat even in this intense heat and tried to pour some between his now rigidly closed lips. After a period of splashing more on his face and because he was now out of the direct rays of the sun, his eyelids slowly flickered and it was very obvious that if we hadn't found him when we did he certainly would have been dead in a short space of time. If Tom had stayed away another few hours or if his car hadn't responded so quickly to my geological hammer treatment, he would have come home to a dead man.

Coupled with the quite different smell of his breath now coming with slow movements of his chest and the curious appearance of his teeth which seemed obvious to be the cause of the stench, I made a bush diagnosis. His whole system was literally poisoned by a mouthful of rotting cavities and this could well have been the reason for his final collapse out there on the fiery hot dust. My hopes for an earlier camp that night faded before my eyes as we both knew that advanced medical help was urgently needed and the nearest would have to come from the hospital at Meekatharra, another 250 kilometres further south. I'd already come that same distance since leaving Ethel Creek that morning but I knew that didn't count for anything now as we carried the almost lifeless body to the house. Mrs Parkinson had prepared lunch by now and thought it would be wiser to eat it before loading the helpless man into my Rover for the long trip. She didn't want me fainting with hunger at the wheel on the way and I reasoned that she hadn't seen me in the Gibson Desert on the most recent expedition.

In any case dinner was a much more hurried affair than I expected, during which the black-toothed one regained enough strength to walk almost unassisted to the Rover and climb into the cleared-off passenger's seat. As this looked like being a long day I headed off immediately, waving to Tom and thanking his wife. He called after me that he would radio ahead to alert the hospital of our impending arrival sometime that night.

In the heat of the cabin it wasn't long before the man from the Kumarina Mine fell unconscious across the middle seat with his breath that much closer and I knew if I did faint at the wheel it wouldn't be for the lack of food. Alternating between life and death the man seemed to be still with me as the sun sank below the skyline and I continued splashing water on his face from a billy.

With the constant sense of urgency and the unwillingness to arrive with a dead body, I discovered I had made quite reasonable time and not long after dark the lights of Meekatharra started showing themselves, not that there were many anyway. A sign pointing to the hospital thankfully appeared on the deserted main street which was in fact part of the highway, and this saved precious seconds of asking the locals, eating in a cafe still open, where it was. In another minute I drove the scruffy looking Rover into the grounds, up a driveway parting manicured lawns, and pulled up outside the main big glass entrance doors in a place I'm sure reserved only for ambulances. In any case right now I *was* driving an ambulance, so letting go of my patient's arm which I gripped when stopping to stop him rolling forward on to the floor I ran up the steps. The hobnailed boots heralded my arrival and a nurse and medical looking man seemed to materialise immediately, thanks probably due to Tom's radio message.

We all eased the unfortunate man out of the vehicle and carried him back up the stairs and into a waiting bedroom. My job was finished but I stayed long enough to satisfy myself he was still with us, filled in an inevitable form, and left him to their mercy. That was the last I ever saw of the man with the black teeth but the doctor reassured me as I made for the door that the act of bringing him in when I did after the long fast drive most certainly would have saved his life and he appeared confident that their hypodermic needles and care would be able to do the rest. They also would contact Tom to let him know that the two of us had arrived both still alive.

Too tired and dusty to think of eating, I drove a kilometre out of the town and camped in the back of the Rover under a mulga tree. It had been a very long day.

Next morning, even though a little later than usual, I went back to obtain some tyres and refuel which brought me again past the cafe and that reminded me just how hungry you can get with so long a time between meals. It was then off east to Wiluna on my way to my own familiar Gunbarrel Highway. I'd be glad to get back to the quiet desert after the problems of civilisation.

The sight of six fluffy little emu chicks being ushered over the road by their devoted father on the 200-kilometre trip to Wiluna made me slow down to make way for them and think what a peaceful family scene it was. I remembered being told that when the eggs hatch the mother goes off leaving the rearing of the brood to the male. After they had safely crossed in front of me I gathered more speed to be on my way again. At that instant a seventh chick who must have been lagging suddenly decided to catch up and shot out from the saltbush under the wheel of the Rover. Stopping and running back I was most upset to see the little bundle of feathers still kicking but beyond help so I took out my revolver and reluctantly put it out of its misery. By the time I reached the little mining ghost town I was feeling very low and told the first man I met about the sad incident. He was Peter Strugnel who happened to be from the Government Pest Control Board and he elatedly assured me I had done a great service to the programme of eradication of vermin.

Quite unconvinced at the 'good turn' I had done for pastoralists in the area, Peter took me on a grand tour of the once-bustling environs of Wiluna. My work on the Gunbarrel Highway had finished five years before another 360 kilometres further to the east at Carnegie Cattle Station, and when that was done we had turned and driven back over it through the Gibson Desert. As usual our work ceased once we had linked our roads to existing access, by which time we didn't have the urge to go any further sightseeing, and so I hadn't until now seen Wiluna.

In years gone by the cattle driven down the Canning Stock Route came to the end of their five-month trip at Wiluna and the holding yards at the railhead were our first port of call. Of course Peter had heard all about our desert activities knowing that I had cut the stock route in several places with my roads. As I looked at the yards I could visualise the bullocks which jostled for water at Well 24 being cooped up within the confines of the railings waiting for the cattle truck ride to the cities.

Well 1 on the route, some 5 kilometres from the town, came next on our list, still equipped with the familiar whip pole and jinny wheel and with the timbering of the hole still in perfect order. The wood had been cut by Canning's party at their first camp at North Well, a few kilometres further out, and boiled for hours to get rid of the sap. Again I looked down the well and at the workmanship which had gone into it and knew what a gigantic task had lain ahead for the party, because when this was done it was a case of 'One down and fifty-two to go'. The ones I had relocated by astrofixes were many hundreds of kilometres distant and those were only half-way along its length.

A visit to 'Cyanide Cyril', as I later named him, seemed at that time to be also a must. He was an old prospector who still wrung out a few traces of gold from the tailings of former mines, somehow using a large tub of cyanide. He stirred the surface with the blade of his penknife, wiped it off on his trousers and offered a chunk of damper to us which he'd cut off with the same blade. For once I didn't feel the least bit hungry.

It was hard to imagine this almost ghost town of Wiluna as a town seething with the activity of over 3000 people ripping up the ground to reveal fortunes in gold only thirty years previously. The peak came in 1933, but it had flourished for twenty years although in the early 1920s the total population was less than 200. As the gold rush gathered in momentum, a railway extension from Meekatharra was completed just before the boom years to cope with the people and production, but soon after the close of the second World War the numbers had dwindled to just over 1000.

The first impression accepted for the derivation of the name of the town was that it came from an Aboriginal word 'Weeluna' meaning the call of the bush curlew, but this was generally discounted later in favour of another word 'Weeloona' meaning the place of the wind. Curlews don't make a call like that anyway. Wiluna also came into significance during the second World War as the Japanese planned to bomb the whole place, for it had gradually become the largest producer of antimony and arsenic in the Commonwealth. The Japanese in fact had at one stage reported that they had already bombed it from the air.

Peter and I, having made the rounds of the area, finally drove to the remains of the once-famous 'Lake Way' Hotel to camp for the night in one of the dozens of empty rooms available. Being the only occupants we had the run of the entire establishment and it was in fact where Peter lived while on his vermin patrols.

All this city living was beginning to take its toll and I was pleased to be on my way early next morning on the 350-kilometre trip north-easterly to Carnegie Cattle Station, the western terminus of the Gunbarrel Highway.

16
A Nostalgic Meeting Place

As I drove away slowly back to the bush I calculated that if all had gone well with the regrading, the party should be at Windy Corner in another three days. It seemed ages since I last saw them out at the McKay Ranges with all that had happened in the meantime, but it had been really only less than a week.

The station road to Carnegie was a well-used access and it was all behind me in one day. There was an exciting reunion in the homestead that night. I hadn't been back since finishing the Gunbarrel Highway there and Roy and Gladys Linke were still in residence managing the cattle station, the same as when we drove in with our bulldozer and grader five years before.

The day after I reached the station was Sunday, and a picnic had already been arranged, so I went along as a matter of course with the entire population of Carnegie; the whole seven of them. It proved to be the hardest day I'd put in since finishing the road to Ethel Creek, for the 'picnic' turned out to be a full programme of roping and branding cattle at a stockyard on a remote outstation. Red-hot branding irons from a roaring fire and the smell of burnt hide and hair filled the otherwise searing heat of the November day as we worked in the choking dust kicked up by the struggling animals.

The best part of the day was the dinner of huge steaks cooked over the branding fire with unlimited brownie cake brought by Gladys, eaten under a scraggy mulga tree, and washed down along with the dust by quart pots of tea.

Back at the homestead with the sun still relatively high in the western sky I noticed one of my tyres had gone down while we had been away and after cutting everyone's hair before their showers over by the windmill, I was able to mend it before joining them. Without any more yarning after tea we were all anxious to crawl into our swags at a very early hour. I had time to remember before I drifted off into oblivion that this day was almost a repeat of my first contact with this station years before and decided that you have to be very fit to attend one of the Linke's picnics.

Heading off quite early in the morning along the still relatively new Gunbarrel Highway I felt completely free once again as I always did after leaving civilisation behind and almost without stopping reached our old fuel dump at the junction where the Gary Highway takes off to the north. After pumping petrol into the Land Rover from one of our own drums left over from our operations, it was here I would be leaving the Gunbarrel on the last leg of my trip to reunite with the party. I was hoping, of course, that on arriving at Windy Corner I would see the fresh tracks of the grader and other vehicles coming from the direction of Talawana and heading north, proving the boys had in fact made it while I had been away.

They certainly had, as I couldn't help seeing on crossing the flat from the last ridge and reaching the junction. There were very fresh tracks in the dusty surface coming from the west and heading off northward. It looked as if a complete regiment had passed the spot instead of the grader and a couple of trucks but it settled the question of what I would do if they had not reached Windy Corner. I had wondered if I should otherwise camp on the area to wait, so duplicating my former confinement out of the raging dust storm only three months before or head off to the west to meet them and help to handle any unforeseen trouble.

Without so much as a hesitation I gladly followed the new dust trail north towards Gary Junction, making new guesses as to where I would eventually catch up to the reliable old party, confident of their loyalty over eight years. Darkness fell when I was not far past the corner and without anything to eat in this extreme heat I stopped under a lone desert oak over by an ever-present sandridge, and was quickly asleep.

The flies decided the time I should be on my way very early next morning and as it happened I had camped one sandridge short of the main group. It took only a quarter of an hour to reach them still camped among the familiar array of trucks and trailers with the faithful old yellow Caterpillar road grader waiting exactly where Doug had switched it off positioned on the road at the head of the convoy. If I had stopped the previous night before the big diesel engine had, I could have heard it easily at that distance but as it was the rest of the then quiet camp had heard me and spent the night wondering why I hadn't camped with them. I was quite pleased with the flies getting me going so early because I was in ample time to join them for Paul's welcome breakfast.

It was a remarkable coincidence that the exact spot of our rendezvous after being separated by a week and over 1000 kilometres, fell right on the centre-line of our original planned flight path of the long-range rockets from the Woomera launching pads, 1400 kilometres to the south-east. It was also in the area of the furthest extent of an expedition we made 'up range' when we had been in the earliest stages of the preparation for the whole, vast Woomera complex just twelve years before.

The day we had pulled out then from headquarters in Salisbury was the old Empire Day, Thursday 24 May 1951, when all the arrangements had been completed for our grand exodus on a three-month expedition into the desert. With all that had happened since that memorable event and looking back on it, it was an unwieldy and cumbersome party of eight Land Rovers, a big supply truck, and fourteen men chosen mainly from the Royal Australian Air Force. This was mainly because the man whom I had taken out on his first trip of relatively short duration and who was to be co-leader was a Squadron Leader engineer by the name of Ken Garden. He had been handling the fitting out of all these vehicles in the H.Q. workshops while I had been winding up surveys for a bombing range at Woomera. This last work had been interrupted by a reconnaissance flight in a Viking air force plane over the country along the centre-line into which we would be penetrating, only three weeks before we were to head off overland. Our pilot had been a Flight Lieutenant who was in the process of converting over to jet aircraft and none of us were to know that almost to the day two years later he was to die in Korea when his jet disintegrated on take-off. Through no fault of his as that accident had been, this reconnaissance flight constituted one of the worst days I think I have ever lived through. Trapped for hour after hour in an oven-like plane, thrown about the sky by the heat thermals off the desert, circling this way and that only metres from the sandridges, I knew in my only partly conscious state that the ground expedition would be easy in comparison.

Half that day I spent in the co-pilot's seat navigating the plane to where we wanted to fly and conditions were barely tolerable, but as we turned for home in the vicinity of my current meeting with the party on the Gary Highway, I surrended my seat to its rightful occupant. I was ready to parachute down to Woomera if the pilot hadn't landed to let me off and a day went by before I was well enough to continue with my surveying of the bombing range.

This was now all in the past when on Empire Day our convoy lined up in front of the H.Q. administration building, the hub of the Rocket Range project in Salisbury. To the excited faces crowding every window in the huge two-storey building we slowly drove out of the main guardhouse security gates to the cheers of 'Westward ho the waggons' from the office workers, typists, clerks, and even the Chief Superintendent.

The object of the whole operation was to explore the completely uninhabited desert country over which the future long-range rockets were due to fly with a view to producing maps of the kind needed to help plan the complex of instrumentation which would be required for tracking the missiles. Also part of this exercise would be to delineate the centre-line as far as possible by actually

Top: Author preparing for night's observation of stars for astrofix with theodolite set-up. *Bottom:* Author calculating results of night's star observation for his position

fixing on the ground, pre-calculated latitudes and longitudes of (at that time of pre-metric measurements) the even 100-mile points along its length. The value of these were given to me by Mary Whitehead, the most pleasant and reliable main stay of the H.Q. maths-services group, using her enormous digital computer. Nothing could be further removed it seemed from a desert battling expedition than this instrument, but such was the nature of this unusual occupation of ours.

My plan was to establish these points on the ground by using a series of star observations and mark them with canvas strips to make them clearly visible from the air. After the long trek we would arrange for an air force photographic plane to fly again over the route and the resulting runs of air photos would show up the canvas markers. They would be then used to produce the necessary maps to plan the future rocket guidance operations.

Three days out had seen us all camping on the outskirts of the most remote sheep and cattle station in South Australia from where the virgin country stretched untouched along the centre-line north-west clear to the Indian Ocean. I had been working in these areas for three years already and I was eager to push out even further but from the outset the size of this expedition worried me. Up until now I had handled this sort of work alone or with one other man, but with every vehicle, more tyres, petrol, and supplies for the drivers were needed and it had snowballed while I had been away.

In any case nothing could be done at this stage and we would see what would happen. The first thing I planned to do was to make a concerted effort to locate an Aboriginal well I had been searching for on and off for years within 100 kilometres of where we had assembled. By digging it out if located, a possible water supply might be available and in this country gold would not have been more welcomed.

While the bulk of the party overhauled their vehicles and rearranged their loads, I took Sam Cheshire, a man who had been working with me for several years already, and another two vehicles to make another try for the well.

Top: Method of ground marking even '100-mile' distances on centre line of rocket range. *Bottom:* From the air these points show clearly on aerial photographs from which maps were produced

It was named Tallaringa on the almost blank map but although I wasn't to know then, it had been plotted by an early explorer 20 kilometres out of position. Aborigines had obviously led him to it eighty-odd years previously and with his sextant and lack of accurate timing, he fixed its latitude and longitude from the stars to the best of his ability.

Being classed as a well I assumed it must be in generally low-lying country and from the top of a sandridge an overall depression could be seen as we stood on the roofs of our vehicles in the direction of the supposed site. Disregarding the old position shown, I made for the lowest country and almost on cue the thick mulga opened up giving way to a very pleasant clear space of saltbush which all sloped to one hollow at its centre. Tallaringa Well had been at last discovered so I camped on the spot to fix its position from the stars for all time, never to be lost again.

We couldn't wait to return to the others and bring the entire camp to the spot to make a united effort to dig out the silted-up hole and if water was discovered, timber it for a permanent supply. The operation would also help in toughening up the members of the expedition who had not spent any time away from the cities. Everyone worked at it with surprising vigour, especially when bones and remains of animals were unearthed as the hole became deeper. Over the previous eighty years dingoes and kangaroos had fallen down the once open hole as skulls and fur came up in each shovelful, and excitement mounted with speculation of further discoveries.

At last at about 3 metres water began to seep into the opening and soon the ones on the bottom who had been filling buckets with dirt to be hauled up by rope were standing ankle deep in water. Success was assured, at least until a sample was analysed in Adelaide months later. It proved to be the worst specimen of water ever examined by the experts at the Department of Mines who couldn't even guess at its source. It was at least washing and radiator water, which was all we used it for after one taste anyway.

After timbering the newly opened well neatly with mulga logs housed into each other with axes and covering it with a lid made of chopped branches, it was time to be on our way again.

We would be separating from time to time as I set about the operation of the astrofixes and marking the centre-line, leaving the others free to cover the general route in search of anything that happened to be there in this previously untouched region.

Almost immediately things began to happen to the vehicles in the thick mulga scrub as they were flogged through the bush and over fallen logs which raked out everything unprotected from their undersides. Oil drain plugs were knocked loose and the hollow brass distorted in such a way as to allow the oil to escape, thus seizing differential gears solid, and the bolts holding springs snapped on impact to cause the axle housings to slide about at will. There are ways of driving through the bush and still care for the normally rugged vehicles but this party had not had occasion to operate in these conditions before. Radiators were staked, side windows broken letting in showers of sticks with every tree brushed against, exhaust pipes torn off so that engines emitted blood-curdling roars as they charged over sandhills, and this was to say nothing of the number of flat tyres as iron-hard mulga-wood spikes tore them to pieces. In short it was just as I had feared and I wondered how long this trip could possibly last at this rate.

With each disaster the driver-mechanics became more and more careful as they nightly licked the wounds of their Land Rovers and almost by the hour the first fury of their attacks on the bush abated as did the casualties. Bitter experience is a good teacher and I could see that our expedition had a hope of surviving after all.

Each Rover had been fitted with a H.Q. designed and manufactured transceiver radio with an elaborate bi-pod aerial array so 'skeds' were held at arranged times with each other occupying hours each day with useless chit-chat. I would tune in every week or so because even out there I was fully occupied in the star work and many of the calculations were carried out after observations at night by the dim glow from a battery trouble light. This was to save water and rations by not camping in the one place any longer than necessary and sometimes I would be working almost all night long to finish the sums.

Being winter the evenings were very cold and even clouds and some rain kept appearing, a condition which was worsened because on the clear nights we couldn't enjoy the usual large camp fires. The heat shimmer caused the stars to appear as hazy blotches through the theodolite telescope making it impossible to read angles to them in that segment of the sky, and my party dreaded the astrofix nights.

The first medical operation of the expedition had to be performed at the 400-kilometre point on the centre-line after establishing its position as the party worked to clear the area. Snowy Newell, one of the drivers, brought his axe down on a mulga tree and a dry stick stabbed his arm leaving a large spike impaled after snapping off short. I used a little precious water to boil up a pair of locking forceps and scalpel and after cutting radial slots either side of the wood, 2 centimetres of blood-soaked mulga loosened and the forceps did the rest.

Kevin Scully was the first to take on the appearance of Robinson Cruso when the bottoms of his trousers rotted off, being already old when they first came out and the ragged ends at knee height completed his wearing apparel for the next three months. He was not only the cook but the proud owner of a cleft palate and he made a great joke of himself trying to pronounce difficult words. The tinned sausages he called 'mysteries' and often on being asked what was on for a meal, a loud reply of 'mitrys' would echo through the sandhills. Snowy once asked him how to spell a long word full of 'S's, and Kev yelled out across the fire his obvious reply of 'I can't even pronounth it, let alone thpell it'.

Weeks of the hardest bush-bashing followed the pattern of astrofixes, sun observations, axework, mending endless flat tyres, mechanical repairs to every nut and bolt on the vehicles, blown head gaskets, water pumps, and of course pulling each other out of never-ending bogs after the heavy rains which occasionally came in winter, even out there. Those rains were the means of keeping our water supply topped up by channelling it into buckets from a canvas camp sheet and we might have been hard put to survive without it.

We had been out for two months when one afternoon as I stopped to observe and plot a sun observation, I happened to look across a spinifex flat towards a low open sandridge to see something I haven't been able to explain away to this day. I couldn't even convince Sam that I had even seen it at all until I showed him the fresh tracks in the sand where I had sighted this apparition. Basically it was an animal but at least twice the size of a large dingo, not quite as big as a calf but with the thinnest stick-like legs imaginable holding up anything of such a body weight. The head hung low on the end of an unusually long neck and after describing all this to Sam, he was sure I'd been too long in the bush again when I added that it was wearing the saddest expression possible as well. I had only a ten-second period to study it as it plodded slowly towards a low shrub, very conveniently as Sam put it so as not to give him time to see it after an urgent shout from me. He just humoured me by asking what colour pullover was it wearing. When he reluctantly walked with me over to the area of my last sighting he at least saw the fresh tracks in the sand but the huge size of them, covering an area the size of a small saucer, completely belied the stick legs. Of course we began a careful tracking operation but had to give up after several hundred metres when it ambled into an area covered by thick never-fail herbage.

I have never lived down the final summing up by Sam of this sighting of a calf-like spectre leaving enormous dog tracks from match-like legs, wearing a fawn jumper behind a giraffe neck supporting a sad face drooping off its extremity. He pressed home his point by elaborately studying a calendar and asking how long it would be before we headed for home.

We were nearing the Western Australian border in the north-west corner of South Australia at the time, near the

800-kilometre point on the centre-line and I began to wonder if the desert was playing tricks. Rabbits were in good supply and we often supplemented our rations by shooting them. On one occasion and looking probably at our roughest, Sam and I photographed each other holding a furry clump by its hind leg, and holding a rifle in the other hand. The picture Sam took of me was published in an Adelaide newspaper many years later where he had successfully applied for a job of press photographer on the completion of this expedition. On the day the picture appeared he nonchantly mentioned to his colleagues that he was the one who took it but nothing he could say would convince them that he was in fact telling the truth.

It was at that stage on the trip that the germ of an idea began to take shape in my mind. If only I had an instrument to convert the rhythmic time signals which were broadcast over the transmitter to give me the chronometer error for the endless star observations for longitude, then a good deal of work could be saved in the long, cold nights of calculations. As the concept of a circular slide rule evolved, I spent any time I had by the camp fires scratching designs in the sand with a stick and with each modification and refinement my excitement grew. I would name the new device a 'Time Vernier Calculator' and had already decided not to patent it because I couldn't visualise anyone else on earth who could possibly want one, but with the vast numbers of such operations I was called upon to do, I knew it would at least help me.

By the time the expedition was finished, I had it completely thought through and with the scribbles in the sand transferred to a field book, the instrument was all ready to be drawn up in conditions much more amenable to those we had in the desert. I knew John Stanier and Frank Chapman in our H.Q. photographic section would print the results, the workshops lathes could turn up the brass work, and I could hardly wait. It was one of the first things I did on returning to Adelaide while the rest of the party were on leave enjoying their recovery from such a hard expedition.

The results of one such star position told us that we

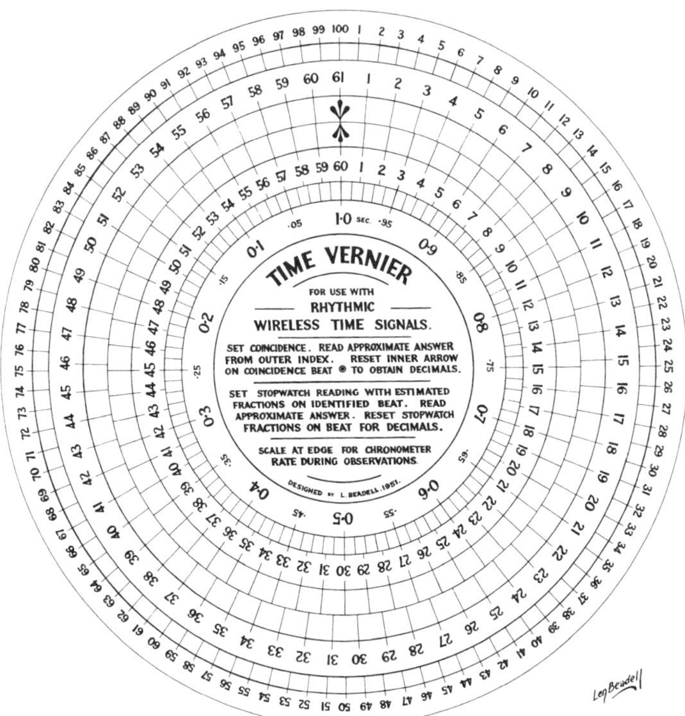

were at last over thc border into Western Australia and were moving in the direction of the place where I had now had caught up to my Gunbarrel boys on the Gary Highway. Little did I know that over a decade would pass before I was in that same area again and that the course of this expedition would be lined by bulldozed, graded roads of my own making, and that this trip was to be the forerunner of the future access into these previously unknown dry, sandy wastes.

Our party had eventually turned a little short of the present position of the Gary Highway close to a point on the Gunbarrel Highway I had named Jackie Junction, and headed back south via the Northern Territory border. We all met near the Musgrave Ranges and passed through the Ernabella Aboriginal Mission to reach the Stuart Highway, then to Alice Springs on our way home.

I also remembered how pleased the members of the expedition had been to finally drive on to the bitumen road leading from the launching pads to Woomera. They had all jumped out of their battered Land Rover as one to kneel down and kiss the tarred surface. Three months of

real bush-bashing in virgin sandridge country would solve the topic of their conversations down south for years to come and Shorty Hicks, one of the air force drivers, still talks thirty years later about his part in the digging out of Tallaringa Well.

Back at H.Q. I had asked 'Sparks' Jarman, our chief radio operator, morse code expert, and wireless mechanic, if he would like to come on another trip with me, and he politely but quickly declined by pointing out 'if you've been on one you've been on them all'.

Since then a dozen years had elapsed and now all these thoughts flooded back to me as I had the best breakfast I'd eaten since leaving the main camp at the McKay Ranges weeks before, one reason being that it was the only one I'd had.

17
Someone Else's Road at Last

Everyone was anxious to be on the move as soon as possible after Paul's breakfast in order to escape the rapidly growing clouds of flies and there was nothing to detain us at our meeting place anyway. Doug led off as usual on the grader having the slowest of the vehicles to set the pace and I went ahead to clear any loose branches which may have blown back across the new road, and waited for him at Gary Junction.

It seemed as though the whole of Central Australia had become our own personal backyard and that everything we were doing was simply adding to something we had already done. Nobody else had yet been on these roads or even knew of their existence since we had made them and as I waited at Gary Junction I thought of the amount of work carried out since I was last on this spot, by far the most remote place in the whole of Australia.

Our next target would be the fuel dump we had established especially for this operation of returning to Giles at Jupiter Well, a further 160 kilometres to the south-east on the road to Sandy Blight Junction. Only one high sandhill crossing would have to be negotiated on the way and Jupiter would be a welcome sight, for the rest of my party had had no chance of refuelling since leaving Ethel Creek, over 800 kilometres behind them.

The steep sandridge barrier was only a few kilometres short of the fuel dump but when the grader eventually reached it, that was where it and the rest of the party were to remain for almost a day as the heavy machine refused to climb it. My Land Rover literally flew up to the top and I thought that at least I could go ahead if necessary to fetch diesel and petrol if anybody finally ran out, as we all had been just about out for some time.

With the grader driven out of the way at the foot of the sandy incline, one of the four-wheel drive trucks also made the grade with a little help from my Rover and a long winch rope, which in turn was able to drag the others to the top. Eventually with all the vehicles except the grader over the crest and tethered to each other with their tyres slackened and with a cable down to the grader, a final effort was ready to be made. The strain on the cables were carefully taken up by the entire convoy with my Rover once again waving about in front until the huge machine began to move up the soft ramp. Nobody relaxed until it was safely up and over on to the level ground beyond. All this was done working out in the blazing late November sun with the sand reflecting any heat which happened to escape us on its way down.

The length of time that operation took was nothing to the minutes it took to reach the fuel at Jupiter Well after rolling up the hot tow cables. In no time all our vehicles were clustered around the drums like a mob of cattle at a waterhole. Actually we were lucky to find enough fuel to see us replenished as it happened, because the Aborigines had discovered them during the long time they had been left there, obviously thinking them to contain water. The thin die-cast bungs on most of them had been smashed in with rocks and the drums pushed over, allowing the precious liquid to drain out into the hot sand. Obviously the disappointed Aborigines discovered the contents to be anything but water. Luckily for us they had given up short of dealing with all of them in a similar fashion, leaving us with just enough diesel and petrol to allow us to continue.

Some 12 kilometres further along the road the Aborigines had again been active. I had carefully chopped a neat survey blaze and installed a rectangular aluminium sign plate with all the information stamped on it to help future travellers who would soon be venturing out into these desolate regions. The blaze was still there as good as ever but it was now minus the shiny plate which had been levered off to be used as a curved carrying dish in lieu of their usual wooden ones. The lubra who owned it now certainly had a prize as they employed these for carrying piccaninnies under their arms. As I stared at the blank space on the tree I could imagine her proudly showing off her new cradle to other members of her tribe. I could also picture one little black body with the latitude and longitude of the area together with the distances to far-off civilisation imprinted in relief and in reverse on its back.

Just as I was about to drive away as the noise of the grader was approaching, a pair of wild-looking Aborigines emerged from the bush and stood grinning at me a few metres away. Even though no words were spoken by either of them they knew very well what I had been looking for, and I knew *they* knew which only made their grin even wider. In the heat of the day and in view of their diesel diet at Jupiter I did give them a tin of water from my almost empty tank before Doug's grader finally bore down on me.

After another fiery camp on the blazing hot open spinifex plains after leaving the sandhill country, I made out a shimmering smudge on the horizon ahead as I churned on in the dust. It was of course the remains of our own ration truck which had burst into flames now three years before almost to the day and in the same degree of heat. The smudge took on a more definite shape as I drew nearer and actually joined itself on to the ground from which it had appeared quite separated by the watery mirage, and I stopped alongside it to relive that exciting day.

Every time we had passed by the burnt-out hulk over the last couple of years we had salvaged some part of it to repair various pieces of our plant and it had been a very handy source of scrap metal on many occasions. One time our four-wheel wooden-tray trailer was in need of a new floor as the heavy pieces of equipment had broken through. The heat-warped steel plating in the back of our old Commer would be just the thing and that involved a day's work with an oxy-acetylene torch cutting out the exact shape to fit. We had cut the springs up for repairing tow bars and although the bulk of the truck was still there complete with its charred engine, there was now little else lying alongside the road where we had dragged it after the flames had died down.

Now it was rusting, even out here with the one or two showers of rain which had fallen over the years but was still too hot to touch, this time only because of the sun.

The camp that night saw us all repairing an assortment of flat tyres which was a standard feature of these sorts of trips as the prolonged slightly higher speeds caused the old embedded stakes of wood to finally penetrate the tubes. The site where we stopped was governed by my fan belt, which decided to give up on a particularly treeless plain and it had been stopping time anyway when everyone had caught up as I was in the middle of replacing it. Lack of firewood posed no problem as nobody seemed interested in adding to the heat in any case and we drank tepid water with the warm contents of tins of bully beef instead of the usual mugs of tea.

It seemed like hours before the sun appeared over the horizon and we were all under way next morning to escape both the flies and the impending heat. In 150 kilometres from the camp we had all reached our old Sandy Blight Junction, which was the crossroads either leading straight on to Alice Springs 500 kilometres away to the east or 400 kilometres south to Giles. All the cumbersome vehicles of our convoy dutifully made the turn to the south with most of the drivers making elaborate exaggerated right-hand turn signals and we were on to the last leg of this mammoth trip of nearly half-way across Australia.

Combined with the very early hour that we had left the last camp and the total absence of any trouble with the machinery, we actually had our destination of Giles in our sights by mid-afternoon and it seemed quite possible to be able to reach it on that same day. By then none of us after the long year's work capped by this trip wanted to prolong it at this stage by even one more day and so our midday lunch became merely a pause for refuelling from the last of the drums and a drink of water. It was homeward bound even at our slow, lumbering pace from then on as the blinding glare from the sun with its relentless heat engulfed our little party, reassuring us that it was determined to remain completely merciless to the bitter end.

At a time late in the afternoon but still broad daylight in these long days, the radio transmitter masts of Giles came into view. It felt like a matter of minutes until it was all over and the simmering engines were switched off clear of the buildings of the Giles Weather Station well before the accompanying clouds of dry bulldust had a chance to settle.

The drains from the bore-water showers were very soon running with liquid resembling cocoa as the dust and sweat was pouring from our red-brown bodies and the huge ex-prize-wrestler cook stationed there was joined by our own faithful old Paul to help in preparing tea. Before going into the mess hut which I had surveyed myself so long before, we unloaded our swags and tended to the bedraggled array of the convoy.

Sitting in the air-cooled mess after tea with the normal inhabitants of the meteorological station, all our stories of the battles with the desert suddenly paled into insignificance as a world shattering news flash came crackling over the little speaker joined to a radio above the noisy gathering. One of the met. boys sitting closer to the speaker must have heard the urgent tones of an announcer indicating an impending dire announcement and had leapt up on to a table to press his ear hard against the wire mesh in order to hear what it was going to be over the din.

The first we heard of it was a raucous bellow from him yelled at least twice the volume of the already ear-splitting racket with the one word 'Quiet!!' Everyone ceased at once as if a switch had been thrown as the man still on the table relayed the news—'President John F. Kennedy has been shot at'—and almost immediately with his ear still glued to the speaker amended it by leaving off the last word—'President John F. Kennedy has been shot!' The very date we had happened to come to the end of our

desert road operations coincided with the day and almost the hour that the President of the United States came to the end of his life. It was Friday 22 November 1963.

The topic of conversation had been suddenly settled and the theories and ramifications of what had happened went on late into the night. Thoughts of collapsing into our swags after the 'day of days' for us vanished as we more and more became aware of what a tremendous difference that one little preposition 'at' had made to such a sentence. While the enormity of this news sank in to our modest assembly in the bush, I'm sure we all secretly agreed that whatever hardships and privations we had endured or could ever hope to endure and were currently recovering from, were absolutely nothing compared to what had just happened to J.F.K. We also realised that the entire world must have been reeling with the shock of the report and it would eventually go down in history forever along with Abraham Lincoln and others. As we ground along towards Giles throughout that day, who would have thought what an anticlimax our ultimate arrival would turn out to be.

Eventually not even this turn of events could keep our heavy eyelids open any longer and we were all asleep the moment we lay down on top of our blankets in the continuing heat of the night.

The next few days were free of anything other than what the boys wanted to do, which consisted mainly of collapsing in the air-conditioned rooms of the station reading and slowly catching up on their suddenly improved diet. That applied to everyone but myself, as the sight of the bureau's typewriter in a cooled room reminded me I had chapter six of my *Too Long in the Bush* written since leaving Ethel Creek. I had already waded through typing the first five chapters and concluded that it would be nice to eventually arrive in Adelaide with everything I had written so far all neatly packaged to present to the brave publisher who had first suggested it. That meant I virtually disappeared for two full days while I slowly clicked away the words letter by laborious letter, only surfacing at the welcomed meal times. Combined with the four chapters done at Warburton and the one at Ethel Creek, the whole six looked quite encouraging and I couldn't wait to see what the experts thought of it. Their verdict would govern the decision to finish the whole book which at this rate would take some time, but compared to the huge projects we had been unceasingly engaged upon for so many years, I felt I could tackle it with confidence.

Then came the operation of preparing the vehicles for the last leg of our migration south to Adelaide, still over 2000 kilometres away. That is, all but the big Caterpillar road grader which was destined to remain at Giles where it is to this day. It was to become a sort of tourist attraction after grading distances approaching 50 000 kilometres on the roads we had made over the previous eight years and we already knew it would be like leaving our right arm behind when we finally pulled out.

A plane was due to land on the airstrip we had sited and made at the beginnings of the station, and as it would be coming the day after we were ready, we decided to delay our exodus to meet the interesting array of visitors listed. As usual we were not sure what they were coming for, as

Top: Jacko, Shorty Bennett, Aub Reilly, and Raggy with newly cut survey line in background for future telephone line to Mount Eba. *Bottom:* Five days after pitching tent it 'sort of rained' and the dry claypan became something else

1951

1952

1953

1954

1955

1956

many such overnight influxes of V.I.P.'s occurred over the years and the reason was invariably explained away by their standard reply when asked: 'We've just come to look around and see what's what!' spoken in an authoritative tone full of hidden meaning far too complicated for anyone else to understand. I'd heard that same sentence word for word from gold-braided high-ranking visitors of every description for twenty years, so I was not disappointed when I asked Air Marshal Sir Edward Grundy the same question as he alighted from the old Bristol Freighter into the furnace-like heat of the airstrip. My old friend Bill Boswell, currently Chief Superintendent of the Weapons Research Establishment, who accompanied Sir Edward was hard put to prevent himself from catching my eye as I put the question to the Air Marshal. Bill had been with me on many identical occasions over the years and studiously kept his head averted when I was told in reply 'I've just come to look around and see what's what!' I'm sure if we had looked at each other we would both have burst out laughing but as it happened as was also always the case, the visitor was a great sport and elaborately discarded his tie and medal bedecked jacket as the heat took over. The yarns of the desert went on until late that night in the mess, as the Air Marshal who had heard of our activities fired never-ending questions and we never did get to know anything about him at all.

Next morning, at an anticipated very early hour, saw us all back down at the strip and the already simmering Bristol and after a hasty farewell, the chiefs and their retinue disappeared behind the gleaming door as it slammed shut and the plane was airborne within minutes. They'd already had quite enough of 'What's What'.

Before the dust churned up by the propellers had settled we were also on our way and it took us all day of grinding through the heat to reach the Aboriginal settlement in the Musgrave Ranges now named Amata, which was a quarter of the distance the Bristol would have travelled in three hours. Although this camp was then known as Musgrave Park it was still very much in its early days, and Aborigines from far and wide were converging on the area as word of

Selection of Christmas cards designed and drawn every year by author, of which around 50 000 were printed each year for the 7000 Woomera residents its establishment spread throughout the north-west reserve. The location of the new community was determined by the discovery of good bore water by geological teams putting down test holes as they drove out along our relatively new road which we had built to establish Giles in the first place.

Two homesteads had been built during the time we had been away and the first superintendent Jim Vickery with his dutiful wife Sheila lived in one and his stock overseer Bob Verburgt occupied the other. Jim had four small children who had already become as fluent in talking to the piccaninnies in their Pitjantjara language as they did to each other. As we related our activities since our last meeting that night I noticed Andy, one of the little boys, take a clear glass jar in one hand outside into the night with its screw cap in the other. After a minute or so he returned with the bottle but this time with the cap screwed firmly to the top and he placed it carefully on the sideboard. Thinking he had caught some insects I took no more heed of it until the next morning when I saw Andy outside in the sun plus the bottle examining it and with a puzzled look on his face, told me it looked quite clear. I agreed with him fully until he argued that it should not be as he had gone out with it the night before especially to capture a 'bottle of darkness'. He explained that it had to be a clear glass jar so the dark could be seen through it!

Mulga Park homestead was the next certain stop to see our old friends Dave and Ted Fogarty, who had started off their station by droving 1000 head of cattle nearly 2000 kilometres from the Northern Territory's 'Top End' with only an Aboriginal and a dog to help them. Dave, the older of the brothers, insisted on getting his ankle broken periodically while horse breaking and currently the same leg was still recovering after the third break causing him to hobble out to greet us leaning on a mulga bush wood stick. Ted had recently indulged himself on a car trip to Sydney and Brisbane and on the spur of the moment over there jumped on a plane to England but not before scribbling a note to Mulga Park telling Dave he was off to see the Poms.

These were the sort of people who formed the backbone of the cattle country in outback Central Australia and no sort of conditions of real hardship would be enough to put even a dent in their everlasting cheerful outlook on life.

Just 150 kilometres further on saw us all at Victory Downs homestead, only 24 kilometres west of the Stuart Highway joining Alice Springs to Adelaide. Once there we would be at last on a road of somebody's else's making. We had been on roads we had surveyed and built ourselves ever since we had left Ethel Creek and Carnegie a fortnight before, over 2000 kilometres behind us.

Victory Downs was where it had all started. Here exactly eight years before we had assembled with our bulldozer, grader, ration and supply trucks, one to keep the machinery moving, a workshop Land Rover full of welding gear and tools, and my survey Rover full of instruments and calculation books. We had begun bulldozing and grading right outside their front door on the project of opening up 2·5 million square kilometres of virtually unexplored Central and Western Australia by the simple process of building a network of 6000 kilometres of road. Of course, we had passed by here on dozens of comings and goings to and from the desert over the years and had always been greeted with open arms by Colin and Pat Morton.

Colin struggled with the work without the help of Aborigines and relied on occasional youths seeking work from down south, and early in our association with him I met one of the prospective new hands at Finke, the nearest railhead 200 kilometres away. He was dressed in brand new cowboy boots, hat, riding trousers, and brightly coloured shirt and as I was driving him out to the station he casually asked where Kenmore Park station was as he had a great friend already working there. I told him it was quite close being the adjoining property to where he was going and wondered why he hadn't requested the city agent for the preference of working there to be with his mate. He looked at me from under the pulled down spotless brim of his Stetson and explained in a most professional wild-west tone with one heavily weighed sentence: 'The judge won't let us be together.'

18
The End of an Australian Era

After the meal of Victory Downs meat while seated at our usual places around their table and with an assurance we would be seeing them again, Colin and Pat were soon lost to view behind a screen of our dust churned up even at the slow pace of our departure. The fact that we were honoured by one of their rare cheerio waves made us wonder which of us was the more crestfallen at the realisation that an era had come to an end. In any case this was not yet the time to be looking back but rather forward to hearing stories of the future use to which the results of our work would be put and the reports from the desert would be heard virtually for ever. We also knew that none of us would have changed places with anyone on earth for the part we had played in it all.

It would have been impossible to bypass Mount Cavenagh homestead on the junction of the Victory Downs Road and the Stuart Highway for a last visit and yarn to Mona, who was one of the first station women we met at the outset and who had been a constant friend throughout. She was regarded in the highest esteem by everyone who knew her, sure of her willingness to help anyone at any time of the night or day. One of the many times Dave Fogarty had broken his ankle, Ted had driven him from Mulga Park direct to Mona's house at midnight after a hard day in the saddle mustering, sure of her help even at that hour. Realising that he wouldn't have a hope of staying awake in the urgent dash to the Alice Springs hospital still many hundreds of kilometres away, Ted didn't even have to explain the situation after waking her up in the early hours of the morning.

One look at Ted's red eyes and the pain on Dave's face and she was in his driver's seat in a flash and with her sorry passengers headed off into the night without hesitation over the churned-up dusty surface of the rough road, and dressed just as she was straight from bed.

She was also right in the centre of the activity on the occasion of the infamous 'Sundown' murders when the bodies of three missing travellers were discovered after a long search, shot to death under a canvas sheet at one of her outstations. The subsequent feeding of dozens of detectives and reporters who converged on her homestead from all parts of Australia didn't shake her in the least from her usual cheerful and hospitable manner. They were camped out on the flat all around her house in swags and to initiate proceedings she had driven the first squad of policemen to Sundown. The sight of the bodies as the tarpaulin was lifted finally did shake her and she for ever after wondered why she hadn't been arrested herself for low flying as she lit out in her utility away from the scene back to Mount Cavenagh, leaving them to get on with it on their own.

As we took our leave of her on that day after more of her tea and scones, we could not have believed in our wildest imagination that we would never see her again. The very dust she had ploughed through for so long on these innumerable missions of charity and hard work proved to be her downfall, and we later wished those sections of the road had been sealed much earlier than they had.

Driving to Alice Springs in the time since we last called on her, ironically to attend a funeral, she attempted to pass a huge semi-trailer to escape the choking wall of bulldust it was stirring up. On a road she had driven over so often and known every scrawny mulga tree on the way, her life came to a sudden and violent end when at a critical moment while overtaking and momentarily driving blind in the dust, an oncoming truck appeared through the cloud a micro-second before that fatal head-on impact.

Not only us but the whole Outback was stunned and saddened as the news spread of the loss of so wonderful a woman.

Camping that night in the bush off the Stuart Highway near Mabel Creek I thought of the way we had begun making another stretch of road from that homestead in the same fashion as we had at Victory Downs. On the first reconnaissance there I had another man with me and during one of the nights of observing the stars for our position he asked me the name of the star I had shown him through the theodolite telescope. After telling him it was known as Beta Fornax, I assumed he must have had some wife or girl friend trouble as I heard his mumbled reply, 'I'd like to beat 'er *with* an axe'. I haven't passed our good friends Ian and Margaret Rankin's Mabel Creek homestead without a laugh at that image of the poor down-trodden, hen-pecked man seeking to escape by coming with me to the bush.

After refuelling at old Ma and Pa Brewster's petrol pumps at Coober Pedy which were the only ones there at the time anyway, we called in for a yarn to Bert Wilson who then owned the only store on the opal fields. He also had the honour of being the father of the lucky boy who had unearthed the opalised bones of a large fish which once swam in the sea covering the Coober Pedy opal fields 200 million years before. At least that was the figure he tried to remember after returning to his dugout home from the experts 'down south', although he did concede that they would 'give or take a year or two'.

The only thing musical about the progress we were making other than the screech of protesting metal and the incessant clanging was the adagio at which we travelled. The further south we went the more frequent were the stops as the distances between homesteads dwindled and it was now only 200 kilometres to Mount Eba, which held special significance to me for two reasons. One was the fact that sixteen years ago at the outset of this whole rocket range scheme, we had been looking very closely at this station for the establishment of the actual launching pads, in which case the whole of the Woomera village complex would have been built there. We had eliminated the idea as that site would have shortened the length of the range line of fire by 150 kilometres and lengthened the return trip to Adelaide by the same distance. With the hundreds of thousands of trips which would have to be made for the future operations in mind, this feature alone would have added countless millions of dollars to the costs in lost travelling time for no valid reason. Also 100 kilometres of rail link necessary to the range head would have to be built against the present 12 or so. The greatly extended water pipe line to supply the town of many thousands of people would need a host of extra booster pumping stations on the way, and these obvious disadvantages ruled out Mount Eba.

The other main significance this next stop held for me was the fact that it lay at the northern end of the Mount Eba line which I had surveyed myself thirteen years before. I had walked the whole 150 kilometres carrying a theodolite over my shoulder in temperatures reading 45°C on my chaining thermometer, taking four months for the operation.

I had been casually asked at H.Q. in Salisbury to lay out a telephone line to be built between our launching site and the current furthest instrumentation tracking station at Mount Eba. The army Line Construction Project Squadron at Woomera would help me with the survey and actually build the line afterwards, so I had attached myself to their camp run by Major Maurie Bennett. As he was too busy feeding his pigs and tending his pet emus, the main stay of the whole L.C.P.S., Aubrey Reilly, was the one with whom I was to have the main contact. Aub, as he of course was known throughout the range, was of swarthy build, tanned to almost black and with an all-encompassing Irish accent when needed, causing all under his rank of sergeant and for that matter all over it, to jump when he spoke—not by any means out of fear but with a willingness to work under him with the sort of savage loyalty he generated in his men. An inventor with numerous patents to his credit, much of the line construction work was reduced to the minimum even to the detail of joining a copper wire to an insulator. With the minutes saved for each of these relatively simply operations multiplied by a quarter of a million, that little instrument he designed alone would have been worth its weight in gold, let alone his sectional steel pole bumper. This tool rammed the segments of each complete post together in two hits instead of the usual one at a time with sledge hammers.

Aub and I got on well together from the first meeting with our mutual dislike for paper work and H.Q., and I carried out some of the first reconnaissances for the line location with him and his family from Woomera in a sort of picnic style. His wife Nel would pack some lunch—with help from Janice and Douglas, his two children aged ten and eleven—and the vital initial surveys would be done under the most pleasant circumstances in my Land Rover. Once when pushing through the mulga scrub belt between the start of the line and Mount Eba, I drove over a hidden stump causing the little vehicle to jolt down violently on its springs and I looked anxiously around to where the children were precariously perched on a box in the back. With a big smile Janice reassured me that everything was all right by brightly pointing out that 'I'm still here!' That same phrase still identifies her to this day thirty years later.

The day finally came when I put in peg number 1 to start the actual survey and we began measuring, reading angles, carrying out sun observations and calculations every night into the early hours of the mornings to keep up with the field work. On Aub's judgment I was allotted two chainmen from the army unit, named Shorty and Jacko, and they were with me to the end four months later. We had the whole unit as a back-up with six axemen to clear the line ahead, and cooks, supply trucks, and helpers laid on to erect camp on the way.

Every chainage had to be compensated for temperature, difference of slope, and tension and a slide rule invented by my old friend John Richmond who had started me off in surveying in the first place and which he called a Versine Calculator helped me with the never-ending reductions.

We had one mountain of a man named big Tagliferri in the axe team and I often saw his great sweaty brown body up ahead literally tearing the branches off the mulgas with his bare hands after bashing at them with his axe which looked like a toy in his hands. This was great until the black day he chopped down a 'special' tree. I had carefully blazed a mulga well off line to spare it from the axe to use as a reference point for a sun observation and spent a particularly long night in my lone tent on the calculations in readiness for a 65-kilometre straight section we were about to run. As I was sighting on the blaze next morning through the theodolite telescope with my hard-earned bearing, I saw to my horror the whole tree totter and

crash to the ground. My reference point was gone and taking my disbelieving eye from the telescope I saw big Taggy standing triumphantly over the stump axe in hand and a big grin on his face. Throwing caution to the winds I rushed over to admonish him, and resembled an ant attacking a bison when I told him he had just wasted a night's work. I knew at once this was all totally beyond his comprehension as his big black eyebrows raised in astonishment at my concern over one tree out of the thousands we had to clear. He had thought it was in the way, not knowing of the plans to put an angle in the line at that point and from that day onwards the area became known as 'Taggy's Tree Bend'.

Cas Hogan, the army cook with the build of a prize wrestler and a feigned temper to match, served up a pie with a difference one day which was as usual applauded by the whole camp. Nobody dared to question what had gone into it and after tea they had all made for their big marquee tent only to discover that every one of their pet galahs normally tethered to their bed heads was missing.

We would shift camp periodically as the distance became too far to travel from the head of the line survey and as the main accommodation for the boys was the marquee a large open area had to be found for it. In advance of the survey I had discovered a claypan of suitable size with a nice surface free of saltbush prickles and decided on it for the site of the new camp. The marquee was duly erected neatly on the smooth low lying surface in this arid country but one weekend when we were all temporarily away, a rare black cloud decided to centre itself directly overhead and divest itself of a deluge of rain. I was quite unpopular when we returned to find the marquee standing sedately in a lake with everybody's boots and belongings floating away on the sun drenched ripples, especially as I had put my tent, quietly removed for my night office work, high and dry on a rise alongside.

One of the most interesting members of the army unit was Phil Davey, a first World War Victoria Cross winner who served on the Russian front. Quite often at night he called out in his sleep stressing that his V.C. didn't make any difference to his role of axeman on the line. As he worked he sometimes muttered the old survey rhyme I told him once, repeating between blows of his axe 'I'll live like a hog, and die like a dog . . . on this doggone survey line'. Phil had incidentally added a Military Medal since to his list of war achievements.

Aub had his own ideas on what he considered to be a false theory about pouring boiling tea into glass mugs, insisting they won't break if filled in a certain way. To prove his point one lunch time he upended the billy, using his special method, into a glass jar balancing on a stone and sure enough not a crack appeared. That is not until he lifted the jar to have a sip, leaving the base still right where it was on the cold rock with the tea cascading down into the sand.

In the early hours of one morning I was awakened by Pat, one of the team, who was holding a towel over his mouth. Asking him what was the matter, he removed the pad to reveal his gaping mouth which he was unable to close. He had yawned and his jaw had locked at the peak of the operation and refused to budge either way. A rush trip back along the line to the Woomera doctor was undertaken there and then to relieve the situation and for the rest of the job if we looked like working him too hard, he would call a halt by simply threatening to yawn.

Day by day the heat from the relentless sun gradually intensified as the end of that year approached, burning us to varying shades of red or brown depending on individual pigments, dressed as we were in only shorts and hobnailed boots. I carried my field book, plumb-bob, and thermometer in a bag attached to my belt with wire hooks, as the usual canvas strap ate into my bare sun-scorched shoulder. Slowly moving for so long in the one direction, I found I was becoming darker on the north-west side of my face.

After an enforced Christmas spell due to the impossible temperatures, the whole team was back on the job with the target of Mount Eba in its sights. The big American six-wheel army truck which the axe party had been using more and more to clear the line by winching the hard mulga trees out by the roots had finally broken down after attempting to tear out a particularly tough stump. They had anchored the back of the truck with a cable to another tree and as the steel winch rope in front took the strain, the whole gearing of the drum flew to pieces allowing Aub to voice his opinion that they had finally killed the goose that laid the golden egg. It had been back to the axes from then on but luckily the survey had broken out into open saltbush plains soon afterwards all the way to Mount Eba.

The last chainage to the terminal peg had finally been

made and the L.C.P.S. could get on with the building of the line and it was only after the whole job had been finished that the decision had been made to construct a good access road alongside for the full length.

Now here we were thirteen years later with the Gunbarrel Road Construction Party returning from the desert for the last time as a unit on our way to Mount Eba, about to complete the final stage of our trip to Woomera on this road alongside the famous Mount Eba Line.

The wheelruts on the road from McDouall Peak, the previous homestead, to their woolshed were so deep that it was possible to drive the whole 6 kilometres without touching a steering wheel. Unlike that road, we found we had to be more careful than ever to stay on the best surface we had been on for a year and still preserve the very close pole strainer wires, and we stopped for lunch at none other than Taggy's Tree Bend. I walked over to the infamous stump and sure enough the rotting remains of the tree were still there complete with my survey blaze and reference mark.

By mid-afternoon the buildings of the air strip at Woomera and the elevated water tanks began to take shape in the heat shimmer ahead on the otherwise bare horizon as our tired array of vehicles and men trundled into the rocket range village.

As I walked into the mess that night I remembered the incident that took place a couple of years before which emphasised just how long we'd been in the bush. It had been in similar circumstances to the present, straight from the desert into a room full of Woomera rocket experts, scientists, and workers all of whom wanted to listen to the latest stories from the never-never.

In that particular crowd a man who was supposed to be well known throughout the world was the current centre of attraction and to whom I was ushered over to meet. Apparently a golf course had been designed for the enthusiasts of the sport on the rocket range by a prominent South Australian gold professional Fred Thompson, the 'greens' being created by pouring countless 200-litre drums of sump oil on to rolled dirt. The president and life member of the Woomera Golf Club, Jack Allan, whose wife Mary was the first woman member, in conjunction with the golf hierarchy had arranged for a visiting golf dignitary to honour the Outback course by actually playing a demonstration round on it with the lucky members.

Affectionately regarded as the 'Father of Australian Golf', this short little man of just over 50 kilograms was in reality a giant of the game who among others fostered the five-time British Open champion Peter Thompson. In the 1940s he won more prize money in Britain than any other golfer on earth, as well as countless Australian Open championships and fifty other tournaments around the world.

The momentous meeting was about to take place as the crowd parted to allow me into the reverent presence of this great man and a hush descended on the gathering as I was introduced. In the awesome silence, Jack Allan's voice uttered the all-important words, never to be forgotten by those present: 'Len, I'd like you to meet Norman Von Nida'.

He looked up at me from his diminutive height, saying as he extended his hand, 'I've heard of your work in the desert—I believe you are an explorer'. If it had been possible, an even more obvious deathly silence enveloped the room after a barely audible suppressed gasp from everybody, at my reply as I shook his hand: 'Yes, and what do you do?'

Probably not one of that group was still in the mess now due to the quick turnover of people at the range, as I clomped in looking just as awkward in the one pair of long trousers I saved for such auspicious occasions and which barely covered the tops of my scuffed hobnailed boots. Nevertheless the throng present did converge as usual to once again listen to firsthand and fresh-from-the-bush stories which always had prompted their questions of 'Why don't you write a book?' For once I could proudly tell them that I had already typed out the great number of six chapters of *Too Long in the Bush* over the last year in the desert to offer 'down south', with a view to finishing the rest of it if accepted.

The same scene had been re-enacted so many times over the previous years that no rehearsal was needed on my part, having so many tales to tell from the country none of them would ever have a hope of visiting. Not that many seemed keen to do anyway as the narration progressed, after hearing their expressions of pain at the conditions under which I worked, and I heard reiterated the well-worn request 'Remind me never to go away on a trip with you!' I always tried to reassure them by pointing out that there just were no conditions. Every individual there seemed to be linked with some episode which identified them for ever and memories were constantly rekindled, some back to the days when I had been first summoned to start it all with a small survey party and a bare saltbush plain.

The next day and in the most disreputable array of tired desert vehicles imaginable, our little Gunbarrel Road Construction Party slowly pulled out of Woomera for the last time as a team, having at last fulfilled the mission on which we had been working for so long. Although not one of us would have dared to admit aloud, I knew that their thoughts would have been the same as mine having camped together in the bush for eight years. The personal satisfaction of having been the lucky ones privileged to be selected to open up for the first time the remaining 2·5 million square kilometres of previously untouched country with our 6000 kilometres of road, could not be put into words anyway. We knew that any development ever to take place in Central Australia in that otherwise virgin area would be governed by the access we had carved into it and that we would have had a hand in moulding its future.

I was also very conscious of the fact that it had taken such an unprecedented project of a rocket range and an atomic bomb test to initiate it all, and if for nothing else, Australia could thank for it the village which was right then melting into the heat haze behind us.

With best
wishes to all
from Woomera – and . .
Len Beadell

Len Beadell, who has been called the last of the true Australian explorers, was born on a farm at West Pennant Hills, NSW, in 1923. After showing an interest in surveying at the age of twelve under the guidance of his surveyor scoutmaster, he began his career on a military mapping project in northern NSW in the early stages of World War II. A year later he enlisted in the Army Survey Corps, serving in New Guinea until 1945.

While still in the Army after the war he accompanied the first combined scientific expedition of the CSIRO into the Alligator River country of Arnhem Land in the Northern Territory, fixing the location of discoveries by astronomical observations. Later, after waiving his Army discharge for a further term, he agreed to carry out the initial surveys needed to establish the Woomera rocket range. It was this decision that was to lead to a lifetime of camping, surveying, exploring and roadmaking in the vast empty areas of Central Australia, opening up for the first time more than 2.5 million square kilometres of the Great Sandy, Gibson and Great Victoria Deserts. He chose the sites for the first atomic bomb trials at Emu and for the later atomic tests at Maralinga.

As Range Reconnaissance Officer at the Weapons Research Establishment he was awarded the British Empire Medal in 1958 for his work in building the famous Gunbarrel Highway, still the only East–West road link which stretches 1600 kilometres across Central Australia.

In 1987 he became a Fellow of the Institute of Engineering and Mining Surveyors (Aust.) and in the same year astronomers at the Mount Palomar Observatory in California honoured him by naming a newly discovered asteroid planet after him in recognition of the road network he created which made access to the meteorite impact craters they were studying possible. In 1988 he was awarded the medal of the Order of Australia in the Queen's Birthday Honours list.

The author of six best-selling books about his experiences in outback Australia, Len Beadell is married and he and his wife have three children, Connie-Sue, Gary and Jackie — all of whom have features of outback Australia named after them.